The Manager's Book of Questions

1,001 Great Interview Questions for Hiring the Best Person

John Kador

REVISED AND EXPANDED EDITION

McGRAW-HILL

NEW YORK | CHICAGO | SAN FRANCISCO | LISBON
LONDON | MADRID | MEXICO CITY | MILAN | NEW DELHI
SAN JUAN | SEOUL | SINGAPORE | SYDNEY | TORONTO

1 2 3 4 5 6 7 8 9 0   FGR/FGR   0 9 8 7 6

ISBN 0-07-147043-3

This publication is designed to provide accurate and authoritative information in regard to the subject matter covered. It is sold with the understanding that neither the author nor the publisher is engaged in rendering legal, accounting, futures/securities trading, or other professional service. If legal advice or other expert assistance is required, the services of a competent professional person should be sought.

> —*From a Declaration of Principles jointly adopted by a Committee*
> *of the American Bar Association and a Committee of Publishers*

McGraw-Hill books are available at special quantity discounts to use as premiums and sales promotions, or for use in corporate training programs. For more information, please write to the Director of Special Sales, Professional Publishing, McGraw-Hill, Two Penn Plaza, New York, NY 10121-2298. Or contact your local bookstore.

 This book is printed on recycled, acid-free paper containing a minimum of 50% recycled, de-inked fiber.

Library of Congress Cataloging-in-Publication Data
Kador, John.
  The manager's book of questions : 1,001 great interview questions for hiring the best person / by John Kador.
     p. cm.
  Rev. ed. of: The manager's book of questions : 751 great interview questions for hiring the best person. 1997
  ISBN 0-07-147043-3 (alk. paper)
1. Employment interviewing. I. Title.
  HF5549.5.I6K33 2007
  658.3'1124—dc22
                                                                    2006004866

To my brothers, Peter and Robert,
for their unwavering encouragement
during wavering times.

Contents

PART III
Other Crucial Interview Topics and Questions   163

Foreword

The proposition that hiring great employees is critical to any business's success is hardly a new message for managers. Whether the critical message comes from Microsoft's Bill Gates or Google's Sergey Brin, the point is clear: one of the most important accomplishments expected of managers is the selection of top-performing employees. But even though managers in every size of business from start-ups to global firms all understand the importance of selecting the very best employees, few can honestly say they have been consistently successful.

WHY MANAGERS SELECT THE WRONG PEOPLE

The primary reason why many managers mismanage the selection process is that they almost always approach the hiring and interview process informally. Why is it that the same managers who develop rigorous processes to deal with financial, supply chain, or customer service issues approach hiring in a decidedly nonrigorous manner? Rather than having precise processes and tools, they approach each candidate and each interview differently, relying on first impressions and their "gut instinct," which they believe is reliable. The net result of this approach is that they make unreliable decisions, resulting in the wrong candidate being selected for the job at hand.

Most managers believe they can identify the ideal job candidate on the basis of an attitude that's best expressed as "I'll know them when I see them!" Unfortunately, my research demonstrates that the more precise or structured the interview and hiring process is, the more reliable the result will be. Yes, I know that many managers initially hate the idea of structure, but they also hate failure, and if they don't structure their interview with the right questions for the right job, they are essentially guaranteeing that their decisions will be less than optimum. Incidentally, not only does hiring the wrong person have immediate consequences in that the new hire will need additional training and supervision, it also means that the new hire will likely fail on the job. The result? The flawed process has to be repeated a few months later.

GREAT HIRING REQUIRES PREPARATION

The key lesson to be learned here is that you should not begin hiring without putting some structure into your hiring and interview process. Start by using the best sources in order to find the top candidates (referrals from current employees, professional events, and your company's Web site are generally the best sources). Next comes the most critical step: developing or selecting interview questions that fit your company, its unique culture, and the particulars of the job to be filled.

Don't use generic questions unless you want to recruit generic candidates. For example, ask yourself, "Would I use the same set of questions to select a brain surgeon as I would to select a gardener?" Of course not, and the same reasoning is true for every type of job that you are hiring for. The key to success is to identify and ask the appropriate questions for the specific skill set that you need for a particular job. Next, compile a list of what you consider to be good, better, and best answers for each question, and then use the list as a script against which to select your finalist. I would offer one additional suggestion: also consider giving candidates a business problem (one that they are likely to face) to solve, as both Microsoft and Google do. If the candidates walk you through the steps they would take to solve the problem correctly, without omitting any critical ones, you have found your new hire.

THE WORLD OF HIRING HAS CHANGED DRAMATICALLY

If you have already developed a set of interview questions, I urge you to continually update it because the environment of hiring and interviewing has changed dramatically over the last decade. Some of those key changes that you need to be aware of include the following:

> ➤ The growth of the Internet has led to a proliferation of Web sites that

offer applicants advice on how to script and answer any commonly used, generic interview questions that they might come across. This means that if you repeat questions or use generalized interview questions, you will almost assuredly be fooled by a group of well-rehearsed applicants.

➤ The speed of change in business has accelerated so much that asking individuals "What were you doing two years ago?" might produce answers that include approaches which would not be appropriate for the current business environment. Instead, managers must constantly update their list of interview questions, and they should expect candidates to give current and relevant answers that reflect the latest tools, best practices, and technologies.

➤ The globalization of business and business processes means that hiring now involves screening candidates who could be from almost anywhere in the world. Update your interview questions to fit the business customs and culture of the country in which or from which you are hiring.

Again, the lesson to be learned is that if you want to hire the best people, you need to constantly revise and update your interview process and questions.

John Kador has been a well-recognized proponent of better hiring practices for years. In this revision of his benchmark work, he updates his classic list of interview questions to meet the changing needs of hiring managers and recruiters. In this edition, he has not only expanded the number of interview questions but he has also added some new categories including questions for exit interviews and questions for considering candidates' ethics. It's a helpful and valuable tool; I urge you to use it.

Dr. John Sullivan
Professor of Management
San Francisco State University
San Francisco, CA
May 2006

Introduction

INTERVIEWING: A SERIOUS BUSINESS

Since the original publication of *The Manager's Book of Questions* in 1997, the job recruitment environment has seen considerable transformation. This book has been revised to reflect the disruptive forces that both recruiters and candidates now confront.

When the book was first published, the business world was just building up to what eventually became the dot-com frenzy. It was a market where even mediocre applicants had multiple job offers complete with signing bonuses and leases to BMWs. Those days, quite simply, are over. Today, dozens of highly qualified applicants compete for every job opening. The power has shifted from the applicant to the hiring authority. That's good for the hiring authority, but with increased power comes increased responsibility. A confusing sweep of structural, cultural, economic, and legal considerations makes selecting employees and team members more critical—and at the same time more difficult than ever before. This new, completely revised edition focuses on the new reality of recruiting.

Gone are the days when human resources took life-cycle control for hiring an employee. Today, more often than not, HR qualifies applicants but then turns them over to a mix of managers, staff members, and even contractors for a bewildering assortment of interviews. At other times, the candidate makes initial contact with the company with the hiring authority who interviews him or her and then turns the candidate over to HR for further processing.

As screening and hiring decisions once administered by human resources professionals are dispersed throughout the enterprise, ordinary employees are called on to make hiring recommendations, and many employees are given short notice to participate in job interviews with prospective employees. These encounters take the form of one-to-one inter-actions or group interviews. The needs of these managers for quick help with job interviews have always been the central promise of *The Manager's Book of Questions*.

This revised edition includes most of the material from the original book but also adds new categories of interview questions. For example, with business ethics assuming new importance in the wake of the accounting scandals and the Sarbanes-Oxley regulations, readers will find a list of probing questions designed to elicit the candidates' attitudes about business ethics. (The Sarbanes-Oxley Act of 2002 imposes rigorous requirements on the practice of corporate governance, financial disclosure, and public accounting.) Readers will also find a list of questions for exit interviews, which many corporations now conduct when valued employees decide to resign. In all, this book not only expands on the 751 questions offered in the original book but delivers more than the 1,001 interview questions promised in the revised edition.

It has not escaped the notice of many recruiters today that the interviewees are better prepared than the managers who interview them. The fact is that many managers and team leaders charged with screening and hiring candidates are often unprepared for the task of interviewing. In contrast, thanks to a plethora of books, Web sites, and training videos available to job seekers, many candidates are far more primed than their interviewers. Preparing candidates for interviews has become a growth industry. As a result, too many job interviews have become utterly predictable showcases for candidates to parade rehearsed responses to questions that are thoroughly anticipated. And that's too bad, because hiring—arguably the most important responsibility a manager has—is more challenging and important than ever.

The revised edition of *The Manager's Book of Questions* is a surefire way to level the playing field.

SEVEN TYPES OF INTERVIEWING QUESTIONS

Interviewing is more an art form than a science. While selecting appropriate and engaging questions is critical, more important is creating a rapport with the candidate, and then listening to what is said *and* what is not said.

Ultimately, a job interview is a type of impersonal conversation designed to increase the predictive validity of potential employer-employee relationships.

Job interviews involve a mix of just seven basic types of questions:

➤ *Icebreaker and background questions.* These questions are designed to put the candidate at ease. In addition, they serve to verify or clarify credentials. Examples of these types of questions are "In your capacity as _____ at your last job, what was your job description?" and "How long were you at _____?" Their purpose is to place objective measurements on features of the candidate's background.

➤ *Behavioral questions.* These questions assume that past behavior is the best predictor of future behavior. They generally take the form of "Can you tell me about a time when you . . . ?" The more precise the conditions specified by the question and the more precise the follow-up, the more predictive the candidate's answers will be.

➤ *Questions to determine fit.* Determining whether there is a good fit between the candidate and the culture of the organization is perhaps the most difficult part of the interview. These questions attempt to place the candidate in the context of the organization and determine if there is likely to be a workable fit.

➤ *Core competency questions.* Ultimately, a job is about the ability to perform, and performance always requires skills, competencies, and aptitudes. Questions in this category are designed to illuminate to what extent candidates possess these skills. In many cases, aptitude tests take the place of questions. It's not very productive, for example, to ask questions about typing abilities when a typing test provides the needed information much more precisely.

➤ *Ethics questions.* When the ethical behavior of managers at every level is under a microscope, it is important that the ethical makeup of candidates' thinking take center stage. These questions allow an interviewer to consider the sophistication of the candidates as they articulate thorny issues around ethics and the role of leaders in shaping ethical behavior.

➤ *Brainteasers and business problems.* It may be appropriate to invite candidates to demonstrate their analytical and logical thinking skills by solving brainteasers or analyzing pertinent business problems. These questions do not necessarily have a right or wrong answer. They are used mainly to test the ability of candidates to think on their feet.

➤ *Closing questions.* At some point, the interviewer needs to draw the interview to a close. The best question to do that is a variant of "Do you have any questions for us?" although some interviewers actually *begin* interviews with this powerful question.

QUESTIONS YES, ANSWERS NO

Please don't look in these pages for answers to any of the questions listed. You will not find any. I have resisted providing answers to these questions because of my conviction that applicants are better off answering questions in their own voices rather than emulating prepackaged answers. By the same token, I believe interviewers are better off having real conversations with applicants instead of comparing their responses to prepackaged answers. Few of the questions have responses that can be deemed right or wrong, correct or incorrect. The questions are better regarded as jumping-off points for the interviewer to listen carefully—with one's eyes as well as ears—and ask pointed follow-up questions:

➤ Why?
➤ Can you give me an example?
➤ Say more about how you came to that conclusion.
➤ Is that what you still think?
➤ How did it work out?

Keep an open mind. The specific content of the answer is rarely the key element you should be listening for. Resist the temptation to favor a candidate whose answer happens to agree with your own. Observe body language. Pay attention not only to what is being said but to how it is being said. Does the person maintain eye contact? Does his or her voice drop with insecurity? Does he or she fidget? Does the person project confidence? Is there a level of enthusiasm? These attributes of a candidate speak just as loudly as content.

HOW TO USE THIS BOOK

This book is designed to point managers and team builders to proven job interview questions. With this book, readers can quickly and efficiently assemble all the questions they will need to conduct a professional and revealing interview. The questions are organized in the order most interviewers prefer. The interview questions are organized by category in Part I. A subset of the best interview questions can also be found in the 40 self-contained interview scripts customized for specific positions that make up Part II of the book.

Part I categorizes job interview questions by function. For instance, if you are looking for some provocative behavioral questions (questions that take the form of "Tell me about a time when you . . ."), the book aggregates all the behavioral questions in Chapter 2. Moreover, a cross-reference between individual interview questions and the scripts in which they appear will allow readers to see how the question in which they are interested is used in context.

Readers will notice that each script includes an optional brainteaser or a thought-provoking business problem. I want to emphasize that by "brainteaser," I do not mean the discredited stress interview questions and practices of the past, in which candidates were abused by such "tests" as the interviewer's walking out of the room to see how the candidate reacts. The questions in this book are stress questions only in that they require extraordinary thoughtfulness and confidence on the part of candidates. But for exceptional candidates—and the interviewer should hesitate to ask such questions of anyone else—these questions make the interview more, not less, fun. Similarly, the brainteasers allow exceptional candidates to demonstrate how quickly they think on their feet. These brainteasers rarely have a right or wrong answer. Rather, they open a window into the eagerness with which candidates engage analytical or logical problems.

Differentiating among well-qualified candidates is one of the interviewer's toughest challenges. These brainteasers represent another tool that, in the hands of capable interviewers, can aid in separating the well-qualified from the true superstars. Since it is currently out of favor to ask candidates to take IQ tests and other personality-testing instruments, brainteasers are often the interviewer's best insight into a candidate's analytical gifts.

In Part II, each script includes between 15 and 35 questions organized by categories such as icebreaker and background questions, behavioral questions, questions to determine fit, core competency questions, ethics questions, brainteasers and business problems, and closing questions.

Few job interviews benefit from the candidate being asked as many as 15 to 35 questions. The scripts in this book represent a framework from which the interviewer should select one or perhaps two questions from each category. Normally, the essential information that job interviews are expected to generate is forthcoming after 8 to 10 questions with follow-ups. Rare is the job interview that requires more than 10 prepared questions.

While it is always best for a manager to prepare for the serious job of interviewing a prospective job candidate, it is not always possible. Some managers receive last-minute calls to meet with a candidate. In such cases, the scripts in this book will provide the interviewer with a framework that has been designed to make both the interviewer and candidate get the optimum benefit from their encounter.

Interviewers are cautioned to consider these interview scripts as just that: a framework on which unique interviewers build unique conversations with unique candidates. It would be counterproductive to use these scripts to conduct rigid interviews. Interviewers must be prepared to depart from the script to ask thoughtful follow-up questions. In fact, many interviewers inject at least two follow-up questions of their own for each question listed in this book. Thus, if you have two or three follow-up questions supplementing the questions in this book, you might use just three or four of the prepared questions in a single script. To the author, this would be an entirely satisfactory outcome.

Part III concludes the book with a number of chapters covering powerful interviewing topics and provides more lists of questions on specialized topics.

Chapter 8 lists so-called illegal interview questions that interviewers should avoid, as well as some alternative phrasings that may pass legal muster.

What questions of a personal nature of a candidate are you entitled to ask? While specific advice on this critical issue is best left to HR training and legal counsel, Chapter 8 includes a discussion of the principles of asking fair and effective questions as well as a list of acceptable personal questions.

In this day of litigiousness, it is vital that interviewers be aware of the risks of asking questions that are, or can be perceived to be, sexist, racist, ageist, or otherwise discriminatory. But in addition to simply listing the questions to be avoided, Chapter 8 rephrases the question that gets to the legitimate content while avoiding the improper structures. For example, it is improper for the interviewer to ask "Do you need to talk to your spouse/partner before you accept a job offer?" But it is perfectly proper to rephrase the question in this way: "Will you be making this decision alone?" Many questions of a similar nature allow such rephrasing. The bottom line? If you can't make an obvious case for why the question is related to the job at hand, avoid asking it.

Chapter 9 lists questions in the sensitive area of money. It is unfortunate that the culture of job interviews in this country has evolved such that the most important consideration of any job (the salary and benefits) is generally talked about last. The existing taboo about talking about money is so strong that many managers are uncomfortable asking candidates about salary matters. Since most job interviews require that at least some questions be made part of the mix, readers will find Chapter 9 instructive.

A new feature added to the revised edition of *The Manager's Book of Questions* is a comprehensive list of exit interview questions. Exit interviews—informational interviews offered to departing employees—are the flip side of recruiting interviews. If the latter is done properly, there will be less need for the former, as employee turnover will decrease. Organizations committed to learning difficult truths can benefit from conducting candid exit interviews. Managers will find a list of proven exit interview questions in Chapter 10.

Most hiring managers, however, will be asked a wide variety of questions. The interviewer must be prepared to answer such questions as accurately and completely as possible. Experience has shown that the types of questions candidates can be expected to ask are predictable. Nevertheless, candidates who have done their research will frequently come up with a zinger of a question that will challenge any interviewer. Chapter 11—"Questions Interviewers Should Expect to Be Asked"—offers interviewers an opportunity to prepare for these queries. For more of these types of questions, read my book *201 Best Questions to Ask on Your Interview* (McGraw-Hill, 2004).

Chapter 12 will serve as a great resource for managers who are looking to add one or two "zinger" questions to the interview. This chapter will discuss the tricky questions that managers can ask in order to truly challenge the candidate and evaluate how the interviewee handles such unexpected, unique, and thought-provoking questions.

With workplace violence being such a serious issue, anything a company can do to screen out disgruntled or potentially violent candidates becomes critical. This is a discipline that goes beyond just job interviewing and relies primarily on reference and criminal checks. However, Chapter 13 lists questions that may help identify candidates with histories or inclinations toward violence. These questions may be included in the job interview under appropriate circumstances.

Note that every script includes the closing question "Do you have any questions?" It's inconceivable to conclude an interview without a variant of that question. Unfortunate is the candidate who declines to offer a question or two in response to this invitation. Most recruiters look upon such a candidate in worse light than the candidate who shows up late for the interview.

WHY THIS BOOK? TO INCREASE QUALITY AND REDUCE LEGAL EXPOSURE

The Manager's Book of Questions: 1,001 Great Interview Questions for Hiring the Best Person has been revised to be even more helpful in assisting managers in the business of interviewing prospective candidates effectively and legally. This revised edition is designed to enable busy managers to respond quickly when they are called upon to conduct an interview.

Good luck in your recruiting.

PART I

LISTS OF JOB INTERVIEW QUESTIONS BY CATEGORY

This part of the book organizes the job interview questions by topic and cross-references them to the script in which they appear. For example, the question "Tell me about a time when you underestimated a budget and had to ask for additional funds" is a core competency question associated with Script 15, which is found in Part II.

The categories of interview questions are the following:

1. Icebreaker and background questions

2. Behavioral questions

3. Questions to determine fit

4. Core competency questions

5. Ethics questions

6. Brainteasers and business problems

7. Closing questions

1

Icebreaker and Background Questions

Putting the candidate at ease is generally the goal of most interviewers. Thus the initial questions in a job interview tend to have an informal feel. Just as icebreaker ships carve a path in arctic ice to make it possible for other ships to follow, so do icebreaker questions clear the way for other, more difficult questions. Some basic queries about credentials and dates may be resolved easily and quickly by these questions. The ultimate goal, of course, is to stimulate a real conversation between two or more people who have a common objective: to determine if there is a reliable fit in the position at hand for the candidate being interviewed.

QUESTIONS

1. Did you find us/the place okay? (S1)

2. Tell me about a project that got you really excited. (S35)

3. What are your most memorable experiences from school? (S1)

4. What else should I know about you? (S4)

5. What aspects of your education/job do you rate as most critical? (S2)

If a question is used in one of the Part II scripts, the script number is indicated in parentheses at the end of the question.

6. Can you think of a challenge you have faced? How did you deal with it? (S26)

7. What are your expectations of your future employer? (S5)

8. What kind of work do you want to do? (S3)

9. How has your day been? (S1)

10. What did you enjoy least about your last/present job? (S6)

11. What aspects of your current job would you consider to be crucial to the success of the business? Why? (S5)

12. How would your friends describe you? Your professors? (S4)

13. Why do you want to work for us? (S15)

14. How long have you been looking for a position? (S4)

15. If you could make a wish, what would be your perfect job? (S14)

16. What were the biggest pressures on you in your last/present job? (S7)

17. Tell me about your last/present job. (S3)

18. What two or three things are important to you in your new position? (S5)

19. Can you tell me a little about yourself? (S17)

20. What was the least relevant job you have held? (S5)

21. What do you feel are the biggest challenges facing this field? This industry? (S2)

22. What goals have you set for yourself? (S6)

23. What did you enjoy most about your last/present job? (S6)

24. Please take me through your professional career. (S9)

25. What did you learn from your internships/work study experiences? (S2)

26. Based on what you know about our industry right now, how does your

ideal job stack up against the description of the job you're applying for? (S12)

27. What can you do for us that someone else cannot? (S6)

28. Who has had the greatest influence on the development of your career interests? (S7)

29. How was your commute? (S8)

30. How do you know about this job and organization? (S3)

31. How would you describe yourself? (S9)

32. Do you know much about our company/department/team? (S9)

33. Are you familiar with our company? (S8)

34. Would your supervisor be surprised to learn that you are seeking new employment? (S10)

35. None of us is good at everything. What are your major weaknesses?

36. How far can you advance with your current employer? (S10)

37. How does this job compare with others you've applied for? (S11)

38. How do your friends describe you?

39. What important trends do you see in our industry? (S11)

40. In your last/present position, what features did/do you like the most? The least? (S11)

41. How long have you been looking for a job? (S8)

42. What are three words that describe you? (S10)

43. What two adjectives best describe you? (S13)

44. What is the most significant thing you accomplished in your last/present job?

45. What would you say are some of the basic factors that motivate you in your work? (S13)

46. What kind of supervisor is likely to get the best performance out of you? (S36)

47. What would your last boss tell me about you? (S15)

48. What are your long-term goals? (S4)

49. Can you name three things about this company that make you want to work here? (S10)

50. What do you think it takes for a person to be successful in your particular area? (S3)

51. What books and/or magazines do you read? (S18)

52. I've read your résumé and application, but what else should I know about you to make a good decision about your qualifications for this job? (S18)

53. What sort of position are you really looking for? Can you describe your ideal job? (S19)

54. Where do you want to be—and what do you want to be doing—five years from now? (S20)

55. Who or what has been a major influence in your life? (S22)

56. What are some of your pet peeves? (S23)

57. Describe a great day at the job of your dreams. (S16)

58. What are the reasons for your success? (S24)

59. How have previous jobs equipped you for greater responsibility? (S4)

60. What makes you proud of your work? (S27)

61. Are you a self-starter? Can you give me an example of an instance in which you have taken the initiative? (S28)

62. How would you describe your organizational style? (S23)

63. What were the most important projects you worked on at your last/present job? (S30)

64. What are the most important rewards you expect out of your career? (S34)

65. How long will it take for you to make a contribution? (S5)

66. What are your most outstanding qualities?

67. What do you know about our organization? (S39)

68. How did you first become interested in your subject area? (S40)

69. We're all customers. What frustrates you about customer service? (S29)

2

Behavioral Questions

Developed in the 1970s by industrial psychologists, behavioral questions represent a new development in job interviewing. Behavioral questions (often not even framed as questions) typically start out "Tell about a time when you . . ." or "Describe a situation in which you . . ."

Most organizations are moving away from a résumé-driven style of interviewing to a behavioral format. The reason to use behavioral interviewing questions is that the most accurate predictor of future performance is past performance in a similar situation. Unlike traditional interviews, which tend to feature résumé-driven, open-ended questions that candidates can answer in any number of ways, behavioral questions are much more focused and create powerful possibilities for follow-up.

The chief strength of behavioral interviewing is that it holds candidates accountable for their past performance. Even if a candidate is asked a situational question (for example, "How would you handle situation ABC?") that bears a resemblance to behavioral questions, candidates can wiggle out of talking about actual past performance in favor of hypothetical responses. In a behavioral interview, it's much more difficult for candidates to provide responses that are untrue to their character. When candidates tell a behavioral story, a skilled interviewer can easily pick it apart to try to get at the specific behavior(s) that contributed to an outcome. The interviewer will probe further for more depth or detail by asking such questions as "What were you thinking at that point?" or "Tell me more about your meeting with that person," or "Lead me through your decision process." If the candidate has told a story that's anything but honest, the response will not hold up through the barrage of probing questions. The initial behavioral question is important, but the quality of the follow-up questions is critical.

QUESTIONS

1. Tell me about a time when you worked effectively under pressure. (S1)

2. Tell me about a time when you had to meet multiple deadlines in a short period. How were you able to accomplish this? (S37)

3. Tell me about a time when you were creative in solving a problem. (S1)

4. Describe a leadership role you have had, and tell me why you committed your time to it. (S39)

5. Tell me about a time when you persuaded team members to do things your way. (S2)

6. Tell me about a time when you wrote a program/report/strategic plan that was well received. (S3)

7. Give me an example of a time when management had to change a plan or approach to which you were committed. How did you feel, and how did you explain the change to your team? (S33)

8. Please describe your last/present supervisor's management style. (S11)

9. Tell me about a time when you had to react quickly to a rapidly evolving situation. (S16)

10. Tell me about a time when you had to make an important decision with limited facts. (S3)

If a question is used in one of the Part II scripts, the script number is indicated in parentheses at the end of the question.

11. Tell me about a time when you said no to someone who asked you to drop everything to help him or her. (S3)

12. Tell me about a time when a team fell apart. Why did it happen, and what did you learn? (S3)

13. How has your conception of information systems quality evolved over the years? (S36)

14. Tell me about a time when you had to implement an unpopular decision. (S4)

15. Describe the work environment or culture and its management style in which you have experienced the most success. (S10)

16. Tell me about a job or project for which you had to gather information from many different sources and then synthesize the information in support of a business challenge. (S4)

17. Tell me about a time when you were disappointed in your behavior. (S5)

18. Tell me about a time when you used your political savvy to push through a program you really believed in. (S5)

19. Tell me about a time when you had to deal with an irate customer. (S5)

20. Tell me about a time when you delegated a project effectively. (S6)

21. Describe a challenge or opportunity that you identified based on your industry knowledge and how you developed a strategy to respond to it.

22. Describe the options you would consider to find resources for a project or goal if you did not have the resources available within your own span of control.

23. Tell me about a time when you surmounted a major obstacle. (S6)

24. Tell me about a time when you set your sights too high. (S6)

25. If I were to interview your reporting staff members, how would they describe your strengths and weaknesses as a manager and supervisor? (S6)

26. Tell me about a time when you went "out on a limb" in a job. (S7)

27. Describe a situation in which you took a creative approach to resourcing in order to achieve a goal.

28. How do you like to be managed? (S7)

29. What good/bad work habits did you pick up from your first paying job? (S7)

30. Give me an example, from your past work experience, about a time when you had an underperforming employee reporting to you. How did you address the situation? Did the employee's performance improve? If not, what did you do next? (S7)

31. Tell me about a time when you set your sights too low. (S8)

32. Rate your management skills on a scale of 1 to 10 with 10 representing excellent management skills. Provide three examples from your past work experiences that support your hierarchy. (S8)

33. Have you held other positions like the one you are applying for today? If yes, describe how you expect the positions to be similar. (S9)

34. Describe one of the best ideas you have ever sold to a peer or supervisor. What was your approach and result? (S13)

35. What is the most important thing you have learned from your previous experience that you will bring to this job? (S9)

36. If there were two things you could change in your last/present job, what would they be, and how would you change them? (S10)

37. Why did you leave your last job? (Or, why do you want to leave your present job?) (S10)

38. In what ways do you expect your next job to differ from your last/present job? (S9)

39. Tell me about a time when you had a reporting employee who performed very well. The employee exceeded goals and sought more responsibility. Describe how you handled this situation day to day and over time. (S11)

40. Tell me about a time when you had to deal with a particular resource management issue regarding people, materials, or assets.

41. How has your last/present job changed since you've held it? (S11)

42. Tell me about a time when you were tolerant of an opinion that was radically different from your own. (S4)

43. If you could make one constructive suggestion to your last/present CEO, what would it be? (S11)

44. Can you give a ratio to express the amount of time you have worked alone to the amount of time you have worked with others? (S12)

45. Describe a situation in which you were successful in getting people to work together effectively.

46. How effectively did your boss handle evaluations? (S12)

47. Describe the things you consider and the steps you take in assessing the viability of a new idea or initiative.

48. Tell me about a method you've developed to accomplish a job. What were its strengths and weaknesses? (S12)

49. How have you resolved problems you have encountered on major projects, and what were the results? (S15)

50. Tell me about a time when you motivated a team in a unique way. (S12)

51. Describe three components of your philosophy of management that demonstrate what you value and how those values enable you to add, as an individual, to an organization's culture and work environment. (S13)

52. Tell me about a time when you had to make a decision that you knew would be unpopular. (S12)

53. Tell me about a time your knowledge of financial and business operations made a difference in the company's profits. (S14)

54. What were the biggest decisions you made in the past six months? (S15)

55. How have you gone about making major decisions in the past six months, and what alternatives did you consider? (S15)

56. Think of a crisis situation that got out of control. Why did it happen, and what was your role in the chain of events? (S32)

57. Tell me about a time when you initiated an action that brought unexpected results. (S23)

58. What factors are crucial within an organization and must be present for you to work most effectively? (S15)

59. Tell me about a time when you reorganized a department or significantly changed employee work assignments. How did you approach the task? How did the affected employees respond to your actions? (S16)

60. What strategies have you devised to handle employees' resistance to change? (S16)

61. How do you prefer to measure performance? (S16)

62. Describe the way your department is currently organized. (S17)

63. Can you give me an example of a situation you have handled which would demonstrate your ability to supervise? (S16)

64. A manager or supervisor must manage performance and conduct periodic performance reviews. Tell me how you have managed employee performance in the past. Describe the process you have used to give performance feedback. (S17)

65. Can you put into context a situation in which you were involved that required a multidimensional communication strategy?

66. Tell me about a difficult decision you have had to make. (S17)

67. With respect to a time when you had to make a difficult decision, what did you learn from that experience? (S17)

68. Tell me about a time when you were able to convince others that you had a better way of doing things. (S8)

69. Think of something that you consider a failure in your career. What did you learn from it? (S24)

70. Tell me about a time when your knowledge of your position made a difference in the outcome of a situation. (S18)

71. Can you describe a situation in which a crisis occurred and you had to shift priorities and workload quickly? (S18)

72. Give an example of a difficult or sensitive situation that required extensive communication?

73. How do you feel about your present workload? (S18)

74. Some people feel that spending a prolonged time at one job demonstrates a lack of initiative. How do you respond to that? (S19)

75. What are the advantages of staying at one job for a long time? (S19)

76. Describe a situation in which you acted as an advocate within your organization for the needs of a particular stakeholder, during which there was some organizational resistance to overcome.

77. Tell me about a time when you solved a problem in a unique manner. (S19)

78. Give me an example of a time when you used your strengths to achieve outstanding results. (S19)

79. When you have entered a new workplace in the past, as a manager or supervisor, describe how you have gone about meeting and developing relationships with your new coworkers, supervisors, and reporting staff. (S20)

80. Tell me about a situation in which you had to solve a problem or make a decision that required careful thought. What did you do?

81. Tell me about a time when you used creativity in your last/present position. (S20)

82. Tell me about a time when your communication style made a difference in a project. (S21)

83. As a manager or supervisor, one of your jobs is to provide direction and leadership for a work unit. Describe how you have accomplished this in the past. (S21)

84. Tell me about a time when your team made emotional decisions about a particular project. What happened, and how did you handle it? (S22)

85. Tell me about a situation in which you developed an effective win-win relationship with a stakeholder or client. How did you go about building the relationship?

86. Tell me about a specific accomplishment you have achieved as a participant in a team. (S22)

87. Tell me about a time when you had to confront a team member. (S23)

88. How do you know you are doing a good job? (S16)

89. Can you describe a time when your performance exceeded expectations? (S23)

90. Tell me about a time when you had to handle a personnel problem and what you did. (S24)

91. Tell me about a team project of which you are particularly proud. What was your specific contribution? (S31)

92. Tell me about a time when you almost lost a sale and worked hard to get it back. (S25)

93. Describe something you have done to improve the performance of your work unit.

94. When you cold-call a prospect, what obstacles do you expect the clerical staff to put in your way? (S25)

95. Please discuss the culture of your organization, and give an example of how you work within this culture to achieve a goal.

96. When you telephone a prospect, what strategies do you use to get past the secretary or receptionist? (S25)

97. Tell me about a time you adjusted your approach to a prospect based on his or her body language. (S26)

98. Tell me about a time when you followed up with a reluctant prospect and still failed to get the order. (S26)

99. What was the most surprising objection you have ever received, and how did you handle it? (S27)

100. Can you talk about a sales incentive program that motivated you? (S27)

101. What is your definition of *sales*? (S28)

102. Give me an example of a time when you went out of your way to meet an agreement.

103. Can you name an example of how you provided service to a client/stakeholder beyond his or her expectations? How did you identify the need? How did you respond?

104. Can you tell me about a time when you took the steps necessary to resolve a problem when it wasn't technically your responsibility?

105. Can you tell me about a time when you identified a new, unusual, or different approach for addressing a problem or task? (S28)

106. Tell us about how you have handled a dissatisfied customer in the past.

107. Tell us about your experience in dealing with the public. (S28)

108. Tell me about a specific time when you had to change your point of view or your plans to take into account new information or changing priorities.

109. Tell us about a situation with a customer that, in retrospect, you would have handled differently. What would you have done to achieve a better outcome?

110. Can you give me an example of a major project you have worked on that involved communication and writing skills? (S30)

111. Describe something you have done to maximize or improve the use of resources beyond your own work unit to achieve improved results.

112. Tell me about a work situation that required excellent communication skills. (S30)

113. Can you recall a time when you persuaded someone who initially disagreed with you to ultimately see the correctness of your position? (S30)

114. Tell me about a time when you worked successfully as a member of a team.

115. Give me an example of your using strategic thinking at work. (S30)

116. Describe your participation on an IT steering committee. What was the challenge? What was your role? What was the outcome? (S38)

117. Can you think of a time when you disagreed with your supervisor on a tactical matter? (S31)

118. Can you describe a time when you had to analyze a problem and generate a solution?

119. Tell me about a time when, rather than following instructions, you went about a task in your own way. (S31)

120. Can you describe a major project with which you encountered problems? (S15)

121. Talk about a time when you overcame your own mental block or prejudices to make a sale. (S26)

122. Tell me about a job or project for which you had to gather information from many different sources and then create something with the information. (S33)

123. Please tell me about a time when you had to identify the underlying causes of a problem.

124. What would you do if your priorities conflicted with the priorities of a colleague also on the project? (S32)

125. Tell me about a time when you anticipated potential problems and developed a proactive response. (S3)

126. Tell me about a time when it was your job to negotiate a deal. (S32)

127. Tell me about a time when you solved a difficult problem at work. (S32)

128. Tell me about a time when you failed to reach a goal. (S32)

129. Think back to a time when you trained a new employee. Tell me exactly what you did to train that employee and bring the person up to the job's performance standards. (S13)

130. Tell me about a time when you lost/won an important contract or sale. (S33)

131. Describe a situation in which you were a member (not a leader) of a team, and a conflict arose within the team. What did you do?

132. Can you tell me about a specific situation in which you prevented a problem before it occurred? (S33)

133. Tell me about a time when your communication style influenced a decision. (S30)

134. Tell me about a time when you had to make a big personal adaptation to get the work done. (S33)

135. Give me an example of a time when you were assertive and took the initiative to get a particular job done. (S34)

136. Describe a recent situation in which you convinced an individual or a group to do something.

137. Tell me about how you would budget for recruiting. (S34)

138. Tell me about a time when you used your knowledge of the organization to get what you needed.

139. Tell me about a time when you hired/fired the wrong person. (S34)

140. Tell me about a time when you had to assert yourself in a difficult situation. (S35)

141. Tell me about a recent problem in which old solutions wouldn't work. How did you solve the problem?

142. Tell me about your biggest hiring success. (S35)

143. Tell me about a time when you made a suboptimum decision about a project. (S38)

144. Describe a situation in which you were able to enhance the usefulness of information in an existing mainframe system and increase your employer's productivity. (S36)

145. Describe a situation in which you established a partnership with another organization or stakeholder to achieve a mutual goal. What steps did you take to ensure that the partnership was effective?

146. Please describe a time when you altered your own behavior to fit the situation.

147. Tell me about a time when you were required to work with people you had not previously worked with. (S36)

148. Tell me about a time when you really had to pay attention to what someone else was saying, actively seeking to understand his or her message.

149. What would you do if you had almost completed a project and the specifications changed? (S36)

150. Give me an example of a time when you recognized that a member of your team had a performance difficulty/deficiency. What did you do?

151. Tell me about a recent and relevant project experience in which you brought together a team to interpret functional specifications and translated that into a sound technical project. (S36)

152. Tell me about a time when you handled a difficult situation with a coworker. (S1)

153. Describe successful strategies for software testing that you have employed. (S36)

154. Describe the most significant business process reengineering project you have led. What were the results? (S37)

155. Specifically, describe a time when you provided feedback to someone about his or her performance.

156. Describe the central attributes of the object paradigm. How does encapsulation or polymorphism contribute to the technology's effectiveness? (S37)

157. Tell me about a time when you improved the way things were typically done on the job.

158. Tell me about a time when you had to take an unpopular stand on a particular issue. (S2)

159. Tell me about a complex problem you have had to deal with. (S32)

160. Tell me about a time you were unable to meet an important deadline. How did you handle this problem? (S37)

161. Please describe the most difficult task you have ever had to perform using a specific tool, and describe how you managed to accomplish it. (S37)

162. Tell me about a time you were required to make a decision that could have had negative outcomes. How did you make this decision? (S38)

163. What characteristics are the most important in a good manager? How have you displayed these characteristics? (S39)

164. Describe a situation in which you had to ensure that your "actions spoke louder than your words" to a team.

165. Would you still take the initiative on a project if you knew you weren't going to be recognized for it? (S38)

166. Our clients frequently ask for projects to be changed midprocess. Tell me how you have dealt in the past with similar midprocess requests for project changes. (S38)

167. Tell me about a time when you had to analyze facts quickly, define key issues, and respond immediately or develop a plan that produced good results. (S38)

168. Tell us how your research has influenced your teaching. In what ways have you been able to bring the insights of your research to your courses at the undergraduate level? (S40)

169. With respect to your participation on an IT steering committee, what technology did you choose? Why? How did it work out? (S38)

170. How did you go about learning a new skill that was required for your job? (S39)

171. Please tell me about a time when you coached someone to help him or her improve his or her skills or job performance. How did you coach that person?

172. Give an example of a situation in which you failed, and describe how you handled it. (S39)

173. Give me an example of a time when you deliberately attempted to build rapport with a coworker or customer.

174. Can you tell me about a time when you changed your priorities to meet others' expectations?

175. What two or three accomplishments have given you the most satisfaction? (S39)

176. Tell me about a time when you were forced to make an unpopular decision. (S4)

177. If I were to interview people who have been your students, how would they describe your teaching style? (S40)

178. Tell me about a time when you had to deal with a client/stakeholder service issue.

179. What is your basic teaching philosophy? (S40)

180. Describe a time when you had to influence an individual or a group on an important issue. What steps did you take to persuade them?

181. Give me an example of a recent incident in which you took the initiative on a project. (S38)

182. Please discuss a time when you relied on a contact in your network to help you succeed on a work-related task or problem.

183. Tell me about a time when you were unable to complete a project on time. (S2)

184. Tell me about a time when you set and achieved a goal.

185. Tell me about your biggest hiring mistake. (S35)

186. Tell me about a situation in which you were able to find a new and better way of doing something significant. (S21)

187. Give me an example that would show that you've been able to develop and maintain productive relations with others, though there were differing points of view. (S21)

3

Questions to Determine Fit

H ire on competence, fire on fit." That's the experience of most organizations. Companies that put all their eggs into ensuring that candidates have the aptitude to do the job frequently find that those candidates, for a variety of reasons, fail as employees. While competence is indeed an important consideration, it is the part of the candidate's portfolio that can be most easily tested. In contrast, the likelihood that a particular candidate will fit in well with the company's culture is more difficult to determine. That's why when a recruitment decision turns out badly, it usually is not because the candidate wasn't capable of performing the tasks but rather, because, for a variety of reasons, the tasks became secondary to other forces that sabotaged the work relationship. Exploring this dimension during the hiring process is the chief work of recruiters. Determining fitness calls for an assessment of both the candidate as well as the organization in which he or she is expected to succeed. Is it any surprise that the word *profitable* incorporates the word *fit*?

Asking questions to determine how well a person will fit with the corporation and its unique culture gives hiring managers clues as to how successful the candidate will be in the target environment. Fitness questions tend to address these considerations:

➤ Craftsmanship
➤ Commitment to quality
➤ Fit with corporate culture
➤ Passion for work

25

➤ Personality
➤ Flexibility
➤ Willingness to accept constructive criticism

QUESTIONS

1. In your capacity as a _____ at X company, what was your job description? (S1)

2. How do you think your supervisor will react when you tender your resignation? (S14)

3. What motivates you to put forth your greatest effort? (S1)

4. How do you keep your staff informed of new developments and organizational decisions? (S7)

5. Have you ever made a presentation at an industry trade show or seminar? (S38)

6. What kinds of people do you prefer to work with? (S2)

7. Describe the best company you have ever worked for. (S37)

8. What specific strengths did you bring to your last job? (S11)

9. What is the most important feature to you in a job? (S3)

10. Please rank the following from most important to least: (1) job duties, (2) hours, (3) distance from home to work, (4) pay, and (5) work environment. (S3)

11. How do you keep abreast of new developments in information technology? (S36)

12. What has been your greatest accomplishment in a work environment, and why do you consider it a great accomplishment? (S4)

13. Are you required to analyze data at your current job? (S32)

If a question is used in one of the Part II scripts, the script number is indicated in parentheses at the end of the question.

14. How do you feel about your present workload? (S4)

15. Give me an example of a situation in which you had to go above and beyond the call of duty to get something done. (S5)

16. What have you learned from your mistakes? (S5)

17. Many of our clients are frequently in crisis mode. What have you learned about working in such an environment?

18. How do you operate as a team player? (S5)

19. How do you deal with people whose backgrounds and value systems differ from yours? (S6)

20. Do you prefer working with others or working alone? (S6)

21. Do you prefer to speak with someone or send him or her a memo? (S17)

22. What programs have you implemented to build morale among those reporting to you? (S7)

23. What would your greatest business *champion* say about you? (S3)

24. Describe the relationship you feel should exist between a supervisor and those reporting to him or her. (S7)

25. What two or three accomplishments have given you the most satisfaction? Why? (S8)

26. How can we best reward you for doing a good job? (S8)

27. Describe your dream job. (S1)

28. Why do you think you'll be successful in this job? (S8)

29. What past accomplishments gave you satisfaction? (S22)

30. When some managers make a decision, they often feel a need to defend it at any cost or despite new information. Can you describe a time when you changed a stated decision or opinion because you were persuaded you were wrong? (S18)

31. Why have you chosen this particular field? (S9)

32. Of all the work you have done, where have you been the most successful? (S24)

33. Most of us can think of an important decision that we would make quite differently if we were to make it again. Can you cite any examples of such decisions from your own experience? (S32)

34. How did you prepare for this interview? (S9)

35. Why do you think you were successful in your last job? (S10)

36. Can you recall a time when you were less than pleased with your performance? (S10)

37. What do you do to welcome and orient new hires into your department or team? (S34)

38. What has prompted you in past jobs to initiate certain projects? How did the projects end up? (S10)

39. What has been your most important work-related innovation or contribution? (S30)

40. Are you a good manager? Can you give me some examples of successes you have had as a manager? Do you feel that you have top managerial potential? (S33)

41. What suggestions did you make in your last job to improve outcomes such as suggestions to cut costs, increase profits, improve morale, or increase output? (S11)

42. If you have complaints about your present company and you believe they think highly of you, why haven't you brought your concerns to their attention? (S16)

43. What would you like to have done more of in your last job? (S11)

44. How does what you actually do from day to day differ from your job description? (S1)

45. What aspect of this job is the least appealing? (S12)

46. What's one thing that should never be communicated in a memo or e-mail? (S30)

47. What are three reasons for your success? (S12)

48. Which is more important to you: the salary or the challenge? (S13)

49. What do you look for when you hire people? (S33)

50. Which coworker at your last job did you get along with least well? What did you do about it? (S13)

51. What experience do you have that qualifies you for this job? (S14)

52. What do you do when things are slow at work? (S5)

53. What results did you get at your last/present job? How do you know? How did you measure results? (S11)

54. Describe the most significant report or presentation you have had to prepare. (S14)

55. What idea have you developed and implemented that was particularly creative or innovative? (S14)

56. Can you describe a time when you pushed too hard on a prospect to the detriment of a relationship? (S39)

57. What goals have you set for yourself in your career? (S15)

58. How do you see our company helping you achieve your goals? (S15)

59. When completing assignments, what kinds of obstacles do you most frequently encounter at work?

60. How do you define *employee morale*? (S7)

61. The successful candidate for this position will be working with some highly trained individuals who have been with the company for a long time. How will you fit in with them? (S16)

62. What is the most difficult situation you have faced? How did you handle it? (S16)

63. What can you bring to this job from your previous experience? (S16)

64. What do you like the best about supervision? (S16)

65. Can you think of an example of something you have learned from someone else's mistake? (S31)

66. Describe your approach to evaluating risk. (S8)

67. Which aspect of supervision did you feel the most comfortable with? (S16)

68. Who are the motivation gurus you find most interesting? (S27)

69. What aspect of supervision is most difficult for you, and why? (S16)

70. What kind of leader are you? Please provide an example. (S17)

71. Have your team members ever come to you with their personal problems? What limits, if any, have you put on those interactions? (S37)

72. What would your boss say about your performance in your last position? (S17)

73. What qualifications do you have to make you successful in this field? (S17)

74. How do you know when a team has met its objectives? (S8)

75. Have you thought about why you might prefer to work with our firm as opposed to one of the other firms at which you've applied? (S18)

76. What do you like the least about supervision? (S16)

77. What skill has been praised or rewarded in your past positions? (S18)

78. What would you do differently in your life? Your career? (S18)

79. Since you were in the same job for such a long time, you've probably grown very comfortable in it—maybe even a bit stale. How would you cope with a new job in a company such as ours? (S19)

80. What experiences do you bring that involve creativity? (S20)

81. What plan of action do you take when facing a problem? (S37)

82. If you were hiring someone for the job you are interviewing for, what three qualities would you look for? (S34)

83. Do you consider yourself successful? (S20)

84. How would you describe your communication style? (S21)

85. Give me some examples of different approaches you have used when persuading someone to cooperate with you. (S36)

86. Can you give me an example of a time when you received constructive criticism? (S22)

87. What organizations do you see as this company's chief competition? Can you compare and contrast the organizations? (S31)

88. If we hire you, what are the top three goals you would like to see this company/department/team achieve? (S9)

89. What is the most boring project you have ever worked on? How did you do on it? (S37)

90. Explain how you overcame a major obstacle. (S22)

91. How do you handle pressure and stress? (S22)

92. As a member of a team, how do you see your role? (S23)

93. If you were a team leader and a team member wanted to do something in a way you were convinced was a mistake, what would you do? (S23)

94. Is turnover always detrimental? (S35)

95. What are the important qualities a person should have in order to become an effective team member? (S23)

96. What qualities do you have that make you an effective team player? (S23)

97. As a leader, what attributes do you look for in team members? (S23)

98. What can you contribute to establish a positive working environment for our team? (S23)

99. What type of people do you work best with? (S23)

100. You say that one of your strengths is follow-through. When has that made a difference in your work? (S24)

101. How do you schedule and commit to quiet time? (S5)

102. Describe how your job relates to the overall goals of your department and company. (S24)

103. What are the most repetitive tasks in your job? (S24)

104. How do you qualify a prospect? (S25)

105. How do you overcome the difficult periods that face everyone in sales? (S25)

106. How do you deal with rejection? (S25)

107. What strategies do you use to repeat the customer's key concepts back to him or her during a sales pitch? (S26)

108. What is your management style? (S33)

109. Have you ever taken over an existing territory/desk? What was the volume when you started? What was it when you left? (S26)

110. What do you despise about making telephone sales calls? (S27)

111. What has been your most negative experience as a supervisor? (S16)

112. How would you describe your assertiveness? (S28)

113. What's your definition of *customer service*?

114. What three keywords would your peers use to describe you?

115. Speak about the customer's "personal zone" and how you use it.

116. Have you been in charge of budgeting, approving expenses, and monitoring departmental progress against financial goals? (S10)

117. What's one thing we at this company could do to make our customers even more satisfied with us? (S29)

118. What is the customer service attitude at your present organization? (S29)

119. How would you compare your oral skills to your writing skills? (S30)

120. Which aspect of supervision did you feel the least comfortable with? (S16)

121. What are the most difficult aspects of your current job, and how do you approach them? (S30)

122. How important are external deadlines in motivating you? (S4)

123. What has caused you the most problems in executing your tasks? (S30)

124. Recall a major project you have worked on; how did you organize and plan for it? (S30)

125. What do you do to make the people around you feel important, appreciated, and respected? (S31)

126. Have you ever had to fire a subordinate? What were the reasons, and how did you handle the situation? (S33)

127. Why do you think you are a good match for this job? (S15)

128. What risks did you take in your last few jobs? What was the result of your taking those risks? (S31)

129. What decisions are easiest for you to make, and which ones are more difficult? (S32)

130. What would your subordinates say about you—both positive and negative?

131. What would your greatest business *adversary* say about you? (S3)

132. Why do you want to leave your current position? (S8)

133. I'm interested in how you accomplish project planning. What planning processes have you found useful, and how do you go about implementing them? (S33)

134. Give me an example of your working with diverse groups of people, including those with less experience. (S23)

135. How do you plan your time? (S12)

136. Can you describe some projects that were a result of your own initiative? (S10)

137. How do you turn an occasional buyer into a regular buyer? (S26)

138. What do you think is the most difficult thing about being a manager or executive? (S33)

139. What makes you want to work hard? (S22)

140. What would your boss say about you—both positive and negative?

141. Do you have a favorite interviewing question you like to ask candidates? (S34)

142. What one thing would your boss say was his or her greatest problem in working with you?

143. What type of work environment do you like best? (S22)

144. To what do you attribute turnover? (S35)

145. What are your strengths? What are your weaknesses? (S22)

146. Tell me about a time when you had to discipline a subordinate. (S35)

147. Tell me about a time when you made a meaningful difference in the career development of a subordinate or colleague. (S40)

148. How would you describe your ability to work with others? (S36)

149. How important is it for you to learn new skills? (S20)

150. Tell us about a situation in which you made a mistake. How did you handle the mistake, and what was the resolution?

151. What do you think your coworkers would say about your work?

152. How do you cope with the inevitable stresses and pressures of your job? (S36)

153. Define *cooperation*. (S1)

154. Can you relate a confrontation that you've had with your supervisor? Who was wrong and why?

155. What are the biggest challenges you face when you are required to work with others? (S37)

156. What has been your most positive experience as a supervisor? (S16)

157. What do you like most about this job? (S9)

158. Under what circumstances should you bypass your supervisor and go to your supervisor's supervisor?

159. How do you react to criticism from superiors if you believe it is unwarranted? (S37)

160. What would you consider to be the three most significant accomplishments in your business life? (S10)

161. How comfortable are you with change? (S38)

162. What did you do the last time you were asked to submit a report on a situation in which it was necessary to compromise quality due to time and resource constraints?

163. Which computer trade journals do you find most useful? Why? (S38)

164. What kinds of people do you find it difficult to work with? (S2)

165. What would your coworkers say about you—both positive and negative?

166. Give us a situation that illustrates your ability to exercise good judgment.

167. Have you published anything on IT? (S38)

168. What strategies have you found successful in managing unfair criticism? (S39)

169. What do you think your supervisor would say about your work?

170. What do you think determines a person's success in a firm? (S13)

171. If I were talking with your supervisors/subordinates/colleagues, what adjectives would they use to describe you? (S39)

172. Your degree is from _____. What makes you think you would like to (or even would know how to) teach in an institution like this? (S40)

173. Why do you especially want to teach at _____? How do you see yourself contributing to our department? (S40)

174. Describe a politically sensitive situation that you were in and how you handled it.

175. When have you had to adapt in your work? (S36)

176. What is the title of the person you report to, and what are his or her responsibilities? (S17)

177. In instances in which you are required to assert yourself, how do you do it effectively?

4

Core Competency Questions

Competency, as used in this context, refers to the aptitudes and behaviors that are necessary to achieve the objectives of an organization. Competency-based questions focus on the job at hand and the particular areas of competence that are important to a job. Competency questions can take the form of behavioral questions, for example, "Tell me about the time when you . . . ," but the emphasis is rightly on the job and abilities.

The good news is that competency is something that can be measured with relative precision. It's also true that every job can be described in terms of key competencies. This means that competencies can be used for all forms of assessment, including appraisals, training needs analysis, and, of course, selection. The questions in this chapter address such competencies as these:

➤ *Individual competencies.* Personal attributes such as integrity, independence, risk taking, flexibility, decisiveness, and tenacity

➤ *Managerial competencies.* Ability to take charge of other people in such ways as leadership, empowerment, team management, strategic planning, and management control

➤ *Analytical competencies.* Decision making using such tools as innovation, analytical skills, numerical problem solving, problem solving, practical learning, and detail consciousness

➤ *Interpersonal competencies*. Ability to deal with relationships using such means as empathy, communication, impact, persuasiveness, personal awareness, teamwork, and openness

➤ *Motivational competencies*. Attributes that drive the candidate such as resilience, energy, motivation, achievement potential, initiative, and quality focus

QUESTIONS

1. What extracurricular activities were you involved in? What made you choose those? Which of them did you most enjoy, and why? (S1)

2. You'll be required to hit the ground running for this job. How will you be able to handle this? (S39)

3. Which of your courses did you like the least? (S1)

4. Was there a course you found particularly challenging? (S1)

5. How do you deal with unanticipated expenses? Can you give an example? (S15)

6. Why don't I see internships or work study experiences on your résumé? (S2)

7. In college, how did you go about influencing someone to accept your ideas? (S2)

8. Based on what you know of the job market, which of your courses were the most useful? The least? (S2)

9. What advice would you give to a student starting college intending to go into your field? (S2)

10. Why did you decide to go to college? (S3)

11. What does the word *failure* mean to you? (S16)

If a question is used in one of the Part II scripts, the script number is indicated in parentheses at the end of the question.

12. What are the advantages of diversity in the workplace? (S10)

13. Tell me a little about some of your extracurricular activities that would assist you in this job. (S4)

14. Why are you working in a field other than the one in which you have a degree? (S4)

15. What have you done to stay current in your field? (S4)

16. Are you satisfied with the grades you received in school? (S5)

17. Tell me about the most difficult employee situation you have ever had to handle. What did you do about it, and what was the result? (S17)

18. Have you ever received a grade lower than you expected? If so, what did you do about it? (S5)

19. What problems do you have in staying within your budget? (S13)

20. What competitive activities have you participated in? What did you learn from participation in competitive activities? (S5)

21. Has competition had any positive or negative impact on your accomplishments? How? (S6)

22. What's one management lesson you learned in college? (S6)

23. Other than money (which is a given), what do you believe motivates people? (S10)

24. What would you say to an interviewer who suggested that you do not have very much organizational work experience? (S6)

25. What qualities do you have that especially qualify you for this position? (S6)

26. At your last job, how often did you take a survey of customer satisfaction? (S29)

27. What are your team-player qualities? Please be specific. (S22)

28. Have you ever been put on the spot by a professor or advisor when you felt unsure of yourself? How did you handle it? (S5)

29. How, specifically, do you contribute toward an environment of teamwork? (S7)

30. What can you do to promote a spirit of teamwork here? (S7)

31. What has been the employee turnover in your department over the past two years? (S7)

32. Have you ever had to make an unpopular management decision? If so, tell me about it and how you handled it. (S8)

33. Describe your leadership style for me. (S8)

34. How do you measure your success as a leader? (S8)

35. How do you determine which individuals need what training? (S9)

36. What training have you offered other people? How do you measure its impact? (S9)

37. In what respects do you feel you have improved most as a supervisor during the last few years? (S20)

38. What is the value of strategic planning to this job? (S9)

39. What intellectual challenge are you looking for in a job, and why? (S9)

40. What do you do when you know you're right and others disagree with you? (S10)

41. Finish this sentence: Successful managers should . . . (S10)

42. Why do you want to get into this field? (S6)

43. User(s) are complaining of delays when using the network. What would you do? (S38)

44. Tell me about a time when you had to pull a team together quickly. (S7)

45. What does the term *total quality management* mean to you? (S10)

46. If you were to start college over again tomorrow, what courses would you take? Why? (S2)

47. Can you give me three elements of your personal code of ethics for the workplace? (S11)

48. How do you go about assigning and scheduling projects and assignments? (S8)

49. Describe a time when you had to make an unpopular decision. (S4)

50. What were your most memorable accomplishments in your last job? (S11)

51. What is a *message queue*? (S38)

52. What is the most difficult problem you have ever tackled? How did you approach the problem? (S11)

53. How do you manage through delegating? (S12)

54. What does the term *global competition* mean to you? (S12)

55. Most of us can look back on new ideas, new projects, or innovations we feel proud that we introduced. Would you describe one or two such innovations you are particularly proud of? (S21)

56. I see you managed the payroll for three subsidiaries. What was the most difficult part of integrating all of them? (S13)

57. How would you characterize your relationships with your last three supervisors? Any patterns? (S20)

58. If you are hired for this job, how will you approach the first 30 days? (S9)

59. Describe the most significant accounting operations reengineering project you have led. What were the results? (S13)

60. Have you had any experience in applying the provisions of the Americans with Disabilities Act? (S16)

61. Tell me how you go about creating an annual budget. (S13)

62. Let's talk about standards of performance. How would you describe your own standards? What would your subordinates say? What would your boss say? (S19)

63. When you were the marketing manager for _____, what steps did you take in planning the annual marketing budget? (S14)

64. How do you manage others day to day while focusing on the big picture? (S14)

65. Distinguish between planning for the short term, midterm, and long term. (S14)

66. How do you quantify the results of your activities as a manager? (S14)

67. Have you ever completed a formal return-on-investment calculation on a strategic investment? Please provide details. (S14)

68. Tell me about the most difficult sale you have had to make. What did you do to close the sale? (S3)

69. Tell me about a time when you underestimated a budget and had to ask for additional funds. (S15)

70. Did you ever have to restructure your budget in the middle of the fiscal period? What approach did you take? (S15)

71. How would you create a budget in the position for which you are applying? (S15)

72. What process do you use for evaluating the training and developmental needs of subordinates? (S15)

73. What's the hardest thing about being a leader? (S16)

74. Are you a mentor to anyone? Who? What is your philosophy of mentoring? (S16)

75. What does the word *success* mean to you? (S16)

76. Do you think your grades accurately reflect your ability? (S5)

77. How many immediate subordinates have you removed from their jobs in the last few years? (S18)

78. Tell me about an occasion when the team objected to your ideas. What did you do to persuade them of your point of view? (S24)

79. What experience have you had in investigating discrimination and/or sexual harassment complaints? (S16)

80. Tell me what you think would be some good approaches to developing overseas markets during the next three years, especially considering the state of the dollar in today's international markets. (S12)

81. Under which circumstances would you refer an employee to the employee assistance program? (S16)

82. Describe a problem that you solved using employee involvement. (S17)

83. How do you go about monitoring and controlling the use of resources? (S38)

84. Describe your system for controlling errors in your own work and the work of your staff. (S17)

85. Some managers are quite deliberate about such things as communications, development, and motivation. Do you have examples of how you have addressed these areas? (S20)

86. What are your most important long-term goals? (S18)

87. Describe the people that you hired on your last job. How long did they last, and how did they work out? (S18)

88. How many immediate subordinates have you selected in the past two years? How did you go about it? Any surprises or disappointments? (S18)

89. Describe the most significant internal control weaknesses you have ever identified and what you did to remedy them. What were the results? (S13)

90. Do you perform employee salary reviews? If yes, what is your approach? (S13)

91. Some managers keep a very close check on their organizations. Others use a loose rein. What level of control do you prefer? How has it changed in the last few years? (S19)

92. What have been the most important surprises you have received from a particular situation's getting out of control? Why did the situation get out of control? (S19)

93. What experience have you had in resolving grievances? (S16)

94. Sometimes it is necessary to issue an edict to an individual or to the entire staff. Do you have any recent examples of edicts you have issued? (S19)

95. What is a Class D IP address?

96. What specific behaviors do you think might interfere with your effectiveness as a supervisor? (S20)

97. Under what conditions have you been most successful? (S7)

98. How do you get along with superiors? (S22)

99. This position requires a lot of outside-of-the-box thinking. How comfortable are you with thinking creatively? (S20)

100. Some managers are short-fused and impatient in their reactions. How would you describe yourself in these dimensions? (S21)

101. Have you found it helpful to take notes when talking to a customer? (S25)

102. What are the legitimate uses for office gossip or the rumor mill? (S21)

103. How would you handle a subordinate who deliberately went about a task in a way that contradicted your instructions yet was wildly successful? (S21)

104. How do you defend the budget in your present position? (S15)

105. What is one thing a teammate can say to you that is guaranteed to make you lose confidence in him or her? (S22)

106. Name some of the pitfalls to be avoided in building an effective team. (S24)

107. How do you get along with coworkers? (S22)

108. How do you get along with people you've supervised? (S22)

109. Your résumé does not list any job experience in the past few years. Why not? (S6)

110. As a member of a team, how do you handle a team member who is not pulling his or her weight? (S23)

111. Have you ever been on a team in which people overruled you or wouldn't let you get a word in edgewise? How did you handle it? (S23)

112. What are *joins*? Explain the different types of joins. (S37)

113. What have you learned about guarding against groupthink? (S24)

114. Are you able to predict a person's behavior based on your reading of him or her? (S24)

115. Describe your organizational skills. (S24)

116. What are some examples of important types of decisions or recommendations you have been called upon to make? (S31)

117. What experiences do you have in your background that show you are capable of creative risk taking? (S11)

118. What factors would you consider in assembling a project team? (S24)

119. How would you go about identifying customers in a new market? (S28)

120. Through what tools can a committee become more useful or productive? (S24)

121. What actions can a supervisor take to establish teamwork in the organization? (S24)

122. You supervise a group of civilian employees. Your employees appear to be at odds with the uniformed personnel. What steps can you take to improve the teamwork between civilian and uniformed personnel? (S24)

123. How would you describe your problem-solving ability? (S32)

124. What strategies do you employ for finding common ground with your customers? (S25)

125. What strategies have you learned to encourage customers to pay on time? (S29)

126. If I were a prospect, what clues about me does this office tell you? (S25)

127. Can you give an example of how you are able to be positive about a product even when discussing a negative? (S25)

128. What have you learned about using sales incentives to promote sales? (S26)

129. What strategies do you use to plant questions in your customers' minds? (S26)

130. When is it appropriate to ask a prospect, "How much do you want to spend?" (S26)

131. Where do you find your telephone leads? (S27)

132. Have you seen or used our product(s) or service(s)? What did you like or not like about them? (S37)

133. What percentage of your sales calls result in sales? (S27)

134. What are the five most common objections you face, and how do you deal with them? (S27)

135. How do you try to show each customer that he or she is important? (S28)

136. This job requires a large amount of travel. How do you handle the stress of traveling? (S28)

137. How do you approach long-term projects? (S32)

138. What have you figured out about prospecting for customers or developing new markets in cyberspace? (S28)

139. How do you deal with conflicts you have with customers?

140. Name one way in which you have provided extraordinarily good service—above the call of duty—to a customer or client?

141. Describe a situation in which you had to go an extra mile for a customer.

142. Most of us become more astute decision makers as the base of our experience broadens. In what respects do you feel you have improved as a decision maker? (S32)

143. How have you handled customers who take advantage of sales support staff?

144. How do you deal with customers who think they are right even when they are wrong? (S29)

145. What are the advantages, if any, of establishing team goals as opposed to individual goals? (S24)

146. What do you do when there is a decision to be made and no procedure exists? (S33)

147. What strategies have you developed to listen to emotional customers without getting hooked? (S29)

148. What experience have you had in making oral presentations? How do you rate your skills in this area? (S30)

149. When do you have trouble communicating with people? (S30)

150. In your current job, who are your customers?

151. How often do you communicate with the person who receives the output of your work? (S30)

152. Are you prepared to fill in for someone who has different, even lower-level, responsibilities? (S21)

153. Would you describe how you have approached making important decisions or recommendations? With whom did you consult? (S31)

154. Tell me what you have learned about reducing employee turnover. (S31)

155. How do you prioritize your time? (S31)

156. Take me through a project on which you demonstrated _____ skills. (S31)

157. What is your process for setting priorities? (S32)

158. When you are assigned to work with new people, how do you go about getting to know them—how they work and what their strengths and weaknesses are? (S30)

159. Have you developed any special techniques for brainstorming? (S24)

160. When was the last time you sent a thank you note to a customer who didn't buy that day? (S28)

161. Would your subordinates describe you as a delegator, and why would they describe you that way? (S19)

162. What has your experience been with retaining recruitment firms? (S34)

163. Describe a situation that required you to use fact-finding skills. (S32)

164. How many projects can you handle at a time? (S32)

165. Prioritize the elements of a complicated project. (S33)

166. What are *cursors*? Explain different types of cursors. What are the disadvantages of cursors? How can you avoid cursors? (S37)

167. What project management methodologies have you found most effective? (S33)

168. What is your biggest weakness as a manager?

169. In what ways have you improved in your capacity for planning over the years? (S33)

170. What is your ratio of initial contacts to actual sales presentations? (S27)

171. How do you handle personnel evaluations? (S34)

172. What strategies do you apply to working with disorganized colleagues? (S24)

173. Tell me about an employee who became more successful as a result of your management. (S17)

174. How do you go about checking references? (S34)

175. Did you ever fire anyone? If so, what were the reasons, and how did you handle it?

176. In your last/present position, what features did/do you like the most? Least?

177. How many people did you supervise on your last job?

178. What questions would you ask, or techniques would you use, to establish if a particular person were willing to do the job? (S34)

179. How many people have you hired in the past two years? Into what positions? (S34)

180. Have you seen our advertising? Our commercials or corporate branding spots? What seemed to you to be effective about them? How would you make them more effective? (S36)

181. What strategies have you developed for handling counteroffers? (S34)

182. Have you ever not taken a risk and later regretted it? (S24)

183. What's the first thing you look for on a résumé or application? (S34)

184. What programs have you found to be successful in retaining employees? (S35)

185. What are the typical problems and grievances that your staff brings to you? How do you handle them? (S35)

186. What do you think is our organization's strength? Weakness? (S38)

187. What is the most common cause of termination in your experience? (S35)

188. Have you thought about violence in the workplace? What strategies have you developed to address this issue? (S35)

189. I see that you program in [whatever language]. How would you link an indexed field variable to display on mouseover? (S36)

190. How do you test your code? (S36)

191. Given a simple program designed to take inputs of integers from 1 to 1,000 and to output the factorial value of that number, how would you test this program? You do not have access to the code. Please be as specific as possible. (S36)

192. What is the difference between an *interface* and an *abstract class*? (S36)

193. How could we improve the hiring process we are using to select a person for this position? (S35)

194. What is *normalization*? Explain different levels of normalization. (S37)

195. What metrics do you prefer to measure user satisfaction with IT? (S37)

196. Do you use an activity chart to track the flow of the activities necessary to reach your goals? (S33)

197. What is *blocking,* and how would you troubleshoot it? (S37)

198. What is a *deadlock,* and what is a *livelock*? How will you go about resolving deadlocks? (S37)

199. Describe synchronization with respect to multithreading. (S37)

200. What do you see as the most difficult task in being a manager?

201. What is an *abstract class*? (S37)

202. What do you look for when you hire people?

203. Explain different ways of using thread. (S37)

204. What are *statistics*? Under what circumstances do they go out of date? How do you update them? (S37)

205. What is the purpose of garbage collection in Java, and when is it used? (S36)

206. What experience have you had in supervision? (S16)

207. Describe the project or situation that best demonstrates your coding skills. (S37)

208. Describe the project or situation that best demonstrates your analytical abilities. (S37)

209. Give me an example of an idea that you developed, and describe how you "sold" it within the organization. (S37)

210. What was the most difficult programming error that you have ever encountered, and how did you solve it? (S38)

211. Can you give me an example of a skill that you learned on your own—that is, a skill you did not learn in the context of a formal classroom environment? (S37)

212. What have you invented during the past five years? (S37)

213. Is any level of employee turnover acceptable? (S35)

214. Are you an effective manager? Give an example. Why do you feel you have top managerial potential?

215. How do you define your management style?

216. What are *constraints*? Explain different types of constraints. (S37)

217. In your last/present position, what were or are your three most significant accomplishments?

218. What are the elements included in strategic planning? (S37)

219. How will you ensure that the implementation of a plan is consistent with the objectives of the plan?

220. What are the steps involved in developing goals and objectives?

221. What is the relationship between goals and planning?

222. How would you go about establishing a mission statement for the organization that you supervise?

223. Did you inaugurate any new policies/systems in any of the positions you've held? (S11)

224. What has been your experience with major expansion or reduction of force? (S18)

225. Have you helped reduce costs? How?

226. How do you maintain discipline within your department or team? (S35)

227. You have been asked to develop an application for the public to obtain general information about the state government. The application will run in kiosks in state buildings. To facilitate public use, what features might you include in your application?

228. Tell us about your experience in migrating from one application to another. What steps did you take to maintain user satisfaction during the migration? (S23)

229. How would I put my socket in nonblocking mode? (S38)

230. Tell us about a difficult or complex programming assignment you've had. What steps did you take, and how successful were you? (S38)

231. What specific behaviors do you think contribute to your effectiveness as a supervisor? (S20)

232. What has been your experience in developing multimedia applications?

233. What actions can you take to ensure that user requirements are appropriately addressed in the implementation of a new application? (S38)

234. What does the term *time compression* mean to you? (S10)

235. You may be overqualified for the position we have to offer. Do you agree?

236. In what courses did you get your worst grades? Why? How do you think that will affect your performance on the job? (S3)

5

Ethics Questions

It's not easy to probe for a sense of the candidate's ethics by talking about them. Ethics is fundamentally an expression of behavior. Yet recruiters are still obliged to try. The strongest approach is to ask behavioral questions about how a candidate has handled ethical challenges in the past. It may also be helpful to gauge the candidate's consciousness about ethical issues and related topics such as stakeholder balancing and corporate social responsibility.

QUESTIONS

1. Tell me about a time when, by your actions, you made a lasting, positive impact on the ethical culture of your organization. (S11)

2. Can you give me an example of an ethical dilemma that a manager might have to resolve and describe how ethics training could help? (S1)

3. What are some of the ethical implications of criticizing the job performance of a subordinate? (S2)

4. Can you tell us about the last time you dealt with an ethical question on the job and how you handled the situation?

If a question is used in one of the Part II scripts, the script number is indicated in parentheses at the end of the question.

5. What are the warning signs that a proposed business decision may have ethical implications? (S3)

6. What is your opinion about professional success that results from pursuing well-thought-out plans versus success that comes from taking advantage of unanticipated opportunities? Why? (S22)

7. What framework do you apply to test whether a proposed business decision is ethical? (S4)

8. How might you be able to gauge a person's ethical mindset in an interview? (S33)

9. Your boss is going on vacation for a month. Although it isn't in your job description to do so, she asks you to work for another manager in her absence. What would you say and do? (S21)

10. How do you define *business ethics*? (S5)

11. You are negotiating an important contract with another firm that has a reputation for driving a hard bargain. After a full day of negotiating, the other firm's representatives depart for the day. They leave behind a folder that appears to contain key information about their negotiating plans. What would you do? (S6)

12. What are the most common ethical problems that managers face? (S39)

13. What is the first step to ensuring that people in the firm be equipped to recognize and resolve moral dilemmas? (S18)

14. How does an organization best avoid punishing its employees for acting with ethical integrity and moral courage on their jobs when those actions might have a negative impact on the bottom line? (S7)

15. When was the last time you did something solely to help the larger community beyond your family and friends? Do you think you have an obligation to serve the community? (S26)

16. How do you evaluate a business decision in terms of business ethics? (S9)

17. What's the unwritten ethical contract between you and the people that report to you? (S10)

18. Can you describe a time when you were tempted to take an ethical shortcut but then reconsidered and took the high road? (S3)

19. Do you make important professional decisions more decisively now than you did five years ago? When you reverse a decision, is it usually because you have become aware of important new information or because you have a change of heart?

20. How do you balance the competing needs of shareholders, employees, customers, partners, and the community and/or environment? (S30)

21. You discover that a recently hired colleague is earning much more in salary than you earn. What do you do? (S14)

22. Tell me about a situation that would exemplify your integrity.

23. Describe your previous employer's strategy for managing ethics. (S15)

24. What do you think about the *balanced-scorecard approach* to corporate social responsibility? (S16)

25. Who should be responsible for ethics in the company? (S17)

26. How important is it to have a values statement? What should the values statement include? (S36)

27. In general, are people in organizations provided with a safe opportunity to discuss ethical issues of concern? What are some ways to promote such safe opportunities? (S19)

28. You determine that a problem employee must be dismissed. Do you provide minimum or maximum notice to the employee? Why? (S20)

29. Is honesty *always* the best policy? (S8)

30. How do you differentiate between fairness and justice? (S21)

31. What are the three most important ethical contributions you have made to a team or organization with which you have been associated? (S4)

32. Which organization in your life has earned your deepest sense of loyalty? What ties you to that organization's principles and activities? (S23)

33. If you knew that millions of people would model their lives after yours, would you change anything about the way you live? When have you changed your behavior to try to influence someone else? (S24)

34. When you make a decision, are you generally more concerned about its immediate impact or its long-range consequences? How much have you changed in this regard during the past decade? (S25)

35. Can business ethics really be taught? (S7)

36. Your supervisor tells you to do something in a manner you are convinced is dead wrong. What would you do? (S12)

37. Do you think you have a better reputation in your professional or personal dealings? (S28)

38. How do you see the difference between business ethics and business social responsibility? (S1)

39. How do you include business ethics into the mix when recruiting? (S31)

40. If two managers give you two projects to be completed by the end of the day and you have time to do only one, how do you proceed? (S32)

41. There are two applicants for one job. They have identical qualifications in every respect. How do you decide? (S34)

42. Why should companies or employees worry about doing things ethically? (S35)

43. How important is it for organizations to publish ethics policies and guidelines? (S6)

44. Can you give an example of a situation in which an employee's actions might not be ethical but are not against the law either? How would you advise the employee? (S37)

45. Can acting ethically increase a company's bottom line? How? (S38)

46. In what ways are your ethics in business different from your ethics in your personal life? (S27)

47. Tell us about a time you handled an ethics issue. How did you resolve it? (S40)

48. Tell me about your morals and integrity.

49. Have you ever spent time at work on personal projects? What would you do to an employee who did this? (S13)

50. In what ways is the Golden Rule an insufficient model for a corporate ethics policy? (S27)

6

Brainteasers and
Business Problems

rainteasers and business problems are not stress questions, although, like all good questions, they may be experienced as stressful. I have little patience for the types of stress situations that some interviewers use to see how a candidate reacts to stressful conditions. These situations include group interviews in which interviewers fire questions at the candidate in rapid succession, demeaning their responses or staring at him or her in silence to see what the candidate will do.

The stress approach often takes the form of argumentative questions or statements. This is an example of a mild stress question: "With your lack of relevant experience, what makes you think you can do this job?" This is an example of a moderate stress question: "You seem much too timid to handle these responsibilities. Is that true?" And this is an example of a major stress question: "That is the worst answer we've heard from any of the candidates. What do you think about that?" Thankfully, such stress techniques are increasingly rare.

Most organizations realize that stress is not productive and is a turnoff to employees and candidates alike. Rather than recruiting people who can work under stressful conditions, most organizations appropriately put their energy into creating work environments that are as stress free as possible.

The information in this chapter is excerpted from my book *How to Ace the Brainteaser Job Interview*, McGraw-Hill, 2003.

That said, there is room under certain circumstances for interview questions, such as brainteasers, that may be considered stressful. When a position calls for high levels of creativity and analytical reasoning, a well-crafted brainteaser or thought-provoking question may give the recruiter some useful insight.

Interviewers are looking for meaningful, uncontroversial conversations with candidates that will provide actionable information on which to make reliable selection decisions. Interviewers hope that puzzles and brainteasers will help create the possibility for such productive conversations.

For certain highly qualified candidates competing for highly analytical positions—programming, systems analysis, consulting—brainteasers offer recruiters some benefits. A well-crafted and elegant brainteaser can catalyze a conversation that can give the recruiter some important information about how the candidates handle a challenge in real time.

A word of caution about adding brainteasers to the mix of interview questions: try to select puzzles that have some relevance to the job and the candidates' real-world business performance. There is a correlation between specific puzzles and real-world skill sets called on by specific jobs because many of the cognitive skills needed are the same. For example, selecting candidates for a job that requires aptitude in strategic planning could be advanced by giving candidates puzzles that call on their strategic planning capacities. A search for a product manager who would be required to make a series of high-risk bets on incomplete evidence could be advanced by the use of puzzles testing quick decision-making and probability-calculating skills. The bottom line is, try to make the puzzle fit the job.

Should you be concerned that candidates may have heard the interview puzzles before? Not really. You should expect that the best candidates have prepared for the job interview and may have considered some puzzles beforehand. But just because they have prepared answers for general questions such as "Tell me about a time when you solved a difficult problem," there is still some value in your asking it. By the same token, there is often value in having a candidate consider a brainteaser he or she may have rehearsed.

You should also be aware that the best puzzles are the ones for which there are many ways to arrive at the correct solution. Or there may be an unlimited number of solution sets, and the fun is in exploring a handful of them.

The purpose of using a puzzle is to stimulate a conversation. While a candidate may have memorized a puzzle solution and can therefore go through the motions of solving it during the interview, it would be difficult for him or her to counterfeit a good verbal presentation on the solution to the problem.

Puzzles appropriate for job interviews help catalyze a meaningful conversation between the candidate and the interviewer. It is in this conversation, more than in the candidate's arriving at the correct solution to any particular puzzle, that the value of this part of the interview is realized. The world is full of puzzles, but relatively few of them are appropriate for job interviews. A puzzle that can produce the best possible traction for an interview has these attributes:

➤ *Solvable by at least one satisfactory answer.* The puzzle is meant to be solved. Asking a candidate to consider a puzzle that is impossible to solve is nothing more than a trap.

➤ *Short.* The puzzle statement is clean, crisp, and obvious. Puzzles with elaborate narrations or many conditions are inappropriate. The best puzzles can be solved in less than five minutes, although the conversations about them can be extended.

➤ *Open ended.* A puzzle that has multiple acceptable answers allows candidates to be creative or demonstrate their ability to come up with multiple solutions. Most of all, if there are no right or wrong answers, candidates cannot be defeated.

➤ *Unobvious.* By this, I mean not only that the problem is deep in some nontrivial way, but that it often suggests an obvious first impression that is inevitably wrong.

➤ *Charming.* The best puzzles engage our intellects in ways that leave candidates stimulated. It's hard to define what gives a puzzle this quality, but we know it when we see it. Puzzles shouldn't be arduous. One purpose for using puzzles in job interviews is to have fun while conducting serious business.

➤ *Capable of quick solution.* The most appropriate puzzles can be addressed in less than five minutes.

PUZZLES AND BRAINTEASERS GUIDELINES FOR USE

The following rules and guidelines for the use of puzzles and brainteasers in job interviews are based on feedback from dozens of interviewers, recruiters, and staffing professionals:

> *Test, test, test.* Always try out a puzzle on colleagues and friends before using it in a job interview. Never use a candidate to test a puzzle for the first time.

> *Know the puzzle inside and out.* Never use a puzzle that you don't thoroughly understand. Knowing the "right answer" is not enough. You need to have a deep understanding of the puzzle and every likely solution set, correct or incorrect, and you need to know how to guide the candidate through the puzzle. You are guaranteed to encounter candidates who have a solid understanding of the puzzle. Be sure you don't embarrass yourself and the candidate by giving a puzzle that you do not understand.

> *Make it win-win.* Job interview puzzles must be win-win situations. That is, they must not defeat the candidate. Some candidates will nail the puzzle, and others will need help. That's okay. But don't let a candidate go away feeling defeated or, worse, cheated. Let every candidate emerge feeling like a victor. Ideally, the puzzle will be a learning opportunity for both parties and, in the best cases, even fun. In other words, you need to practice having a meaningful conversation about the challenge.

> *If in doubt, don't.* If you're not absolutely sure about a puzzle or brainteaser, don't even think about using it. Never just throw puzzles at candidates to see what sticks. Make sure you understand what information you are looking for and how you will use the results.

QUESTIONS

1. Can you give me your description of the position for which you are being interviewed? (S1)

If a question is used in one of the Part II scripts, the script number is indicated in parentheses at the end of the question.

2. How would you reinvent our business from an IT perspective if you had a blank sheet of paper and no resource constraints? (S37)

3. Take as a given that you got this job and you have been doing it for three to six months, but things are just not working out. We are sitting here discussing the situation. What do you think you would say about what went wrong? (S39)

4. Different is not always better, but better is always different. Can you describe something you have done that was new and different for your company and that improved performance and/or productivity? (S2)

5. Who is the toughest employer you have ever had, and in what way was he or she the toughest? (S3)

6. How would you describe your management philosophy? (S33)

7. How many candidates for a position does it take to know there's a 50-50 chance that two candidates share the same birthday?

8. What would your coworkers and subordinates say about your management style? (S8)

9. What is the worst thing you have heard about our company? (S12)

10. How has your tolerance for accepting mistakes from your subordinates changed over the years? (S18)

11. How would you finish this sentence: Most people are basically . . . ? (S4)

12. Have you done your best work yet? (S5)

13. How many disposable diapers were sold in the United States last year?

14. What cherished management belief have you had to give up in order to get where you are? (S5)

15. How tall is this building?

16. What was the last product or service you saw that took your breath away? (S6)

17. What's the most significant compliment anyone has ever paid you? (S6)

18. What is your concept of workplace discipline? (S35)

19. Have you ever had a conflict at work that you couldn't resolve? How did you handle it? (S7)

20. Please take this pen and sell it to me. Tell me about its design excellence, features, benefits, and values.

21. What would you do if everyone in your department called in sick at the same time? (S34)

22. You want to go swimming in a pool. The water is a little colder than comfortable. Are you the type of person who jumps in or the type who wades in? (S9)

23. What is the broader significance of your research? How does it expand our historic understanding, literary knowledge, and/or humanistic horizons? (S40)

24. If you could organize the world in one of three ways—no scarcity, no problems, or no rules—which way would you do it? (S11)

25. Consider an analog clock. How many times a day do a clock's hands overlap?

26. Which individual has been a major influence in your life? (S11)

27. How have you been an agent for change in your last/present position? (S12)

28. How would you rate me as an interviewer? (S14)

29. What do you want to hear first, the good news or the bad news? (S13)

30. Think back over the past two or three years and recall a work situation that stands out in your mind as a turning point. Describe what it was, who was involved, what your role was, and what the outcome was. (S13)

31. If your photograph were splashed on a magazine cover, what would the magazine be, and what would the headline say? (S14)

32. When you've had a really good day at work and you go home and kick back and you feel satisfied, what was it about that day that made you feel really good? (S17)

33. How have you benefited from your disappointments? (S15)

34. How would you weigh a Boeing 747 without using scales?

35. Can you suggest three reasons why manhole covers are circular? (S15)

36. Describe a situation in which your work or ideas were criticized. (S16)

37. Finish this sentence: I know I am taking a risk when . . . (S27)

38. Which management gurus do you find most interesting? (S17)

39. On what occasions are you tempted to lie? (S19)

40. How many notes are played on a given radio station in a given year?

41. How has your tolerance for accepting mistakes from your subordinates changed over the years? (S8)

42. How has your perspective of quality evolved over your career? (S18)

43. When I say the word *initiative*, what is the first thought that comes to mind? (S38)

44. What makes you unique? (S19)

45. Here's a saltshaker. Show me how you would test it.

46. What would you like to see inscribed on your headstone? (S19)

47. When is it better to ask for forgiveness than to ask for permission? (S24)

48. The business world is full of euphemisms. What's your current favorite? (S20)

49. Design a remote control for a venetian blind.

50. Should all business relationships have fixed terms—that is, expiration dates? (S20)

51. When you have had a really bad day at work and you go home and feel upset, what was it about that day that made you feel really upset? (S17)

52. Describe a time when you unfairly got caught up in office politics. (S21)

53. What's the difference between a manager and a leader? (S22)

54. What's more important to you, truth or comfort? (S23)

55. How many quarter coins are there in Yankee Stadium during a sold-out baseball game?

56. How would you react if I told you that your interview, so far, was *terrible*? (S23)

57. How much money does the tooth fairy distribute worldwide each year?

58. What are the characteristics of a successful team? (S23)

59. How many gallons of gasoline are used by cars each year in the United States?

60. You supervise a group of employees. One employee complains that the office is too hot, another employee complains that the office is too cold. How would you handle this? (S16)

61. Tell me about the most successful risk you've ever taken. (S24)

62. Can you sell me on our product/service? (S25)

63. Is there anything positive to be said about conventional wisdom? (S21)

64. Are you the type of person that prefers to make lists or the type that prefers to strike items off lists? (S26)

65. Tell me about a boss you did not get along with. (S26)

66. Design a spice rack for a blind person.

67. If you could eliminate one responsibility from your last job, what would it be? (S33)

68. What is your philosophy of mentoring? (S28)

69. Have you ever had a crisis you couldn't deal with?

70. Estimate the total amount of time 19 year olds in the United States spent during this past semester studying for exams in college (not counting finals).

71. If you had the opportunity to do the last 10 years of your career over again, what would you do differently? (S30)

72. An employee continues to make careless mistakes. How will you address the situation? (S30)

73. Describe the most difficult decision you have ever had to make. Reflecting back, was your decision the best possible choice you could have made? Why or why not? (S31)

74. Imagine I am blind. Describe blue to me.

75. How successful do you believe you've been so far? (S31)

76. In your career, what negotiation are you most proud of? (S32)

77. If the land area of the earth were divided up equally for each person on the planet, about how much would you get?

78. What has been your biggest analytical challenge? (S32)

79. Approximately what fraction of the area of the continental United States is covered by automobiles?

80. How many gas stations are there in the United States?

81. Which of your skills can stand improvement at this time? (S25)

82. How would you test the functionality of this stapler?

83. What would be impossible for you to do, but if you could do it, it would greatly increase your productivity, results, and/or success? (S36)

84. Do you agree with the statement that most people learn more from their mistakes than their successes? Why or why not? (S4)

85. If you had to eliminate one of the 50 states in the United States, which one would you eliminate and why? (S10)

86. What is the most satisfying business compliment that you have ever been paid? (S18)

7

Closing Questions

The most important closing question and the one that every interview should include is this one: "Thank you for answering my questions. Now, do you have any questions for me/us?"

Of the following five behaviors candidates exhibit in job interviews, what behavior do recruiters and hiring managers find most unforgivable?

1. Poor personal appearance
2. Overemphasis on money
3. Failure to look at interviewer while interviewing
4. Failure to ask questions
5. Late to the interview

The answer is number 4. No surprise. Candidates who do not ask any questions represent the number 1 behavior that causes recruiters to lose confidence, according to an admittedly informal survey of over 150 recruiters, job coaches, and hiring managers.

QUESTIONS

1. Do you have any questions? (S1)

If a question is used in one of the Part II scripts, the script number is indicated in parentheses at the end of the question.

2. What have you observed so far about our firm and the interviewers you've met? (S9)

3. Is there anything else I should know about you? (S2)

4. I've interviewed several very good candidates, and I will admit that you are one of them. What single message would you like me to remember that will convince me that *you* are the one we should hire? (S8)

5. What do you want to be doing five years from now? (S17)

6. What implications have you drawn from the information you have learned today? (S5)

7. Is there any question I should have asked you but did not? (S3)

8. If there were one reason why we should select you over the other applicants, what would that be? (S7)

9. What are the three most important personal contributions you have made to the last program with which you've been associated?

10. Is there anything you'd like to know about the job that would help you to do it better than anyone else? (S6)

11. Well, based on what we have discussed, how do you feel about this job? (S1)

12. What did you accomplish at work the day before yesterday—in detail? (S26)

PART II

INTERVIEW SCRIPTS 1–40

SCRIPT 1

Entry Level

Icebreaker and Background Questions

1. How has your day been?

2. Did you find us/the place okay?

3. What are your most memorable experiences from school?

Behavioral Questions

4. Tell me about a time when you worked effectively under pressure.

5. Tell me about a time when you handled a difficult situation with a coworker.

6. Tell me about a time when you were creative in solving a problem.

Questions to Determine Fit

7. In your capacity as a _____ at X company, what was your job description?

8. How does what you actually do from day to day differ from your job description?

9. What motivates you to put forth your greatest effort?

10. Describe your dream job.

11. Define *cooperation*.

Core Competency Questions

12. What extracurricular activities were you involved in? What made you choose those? Which of them did you most enjoy, and why?

13. What led you to select your major? Your minor?

14. Which of your courses did you like the least?

15. Was there a course you found particularly challenging?

Ethics Questions

16. How do you see the difference between business ethics and business social responsibility?

17. Can you give me an example of an ethical dilemma that a manager might have to resolve and describe how ethics training could help?

Brainteasers and Business Problems

18. Can you give me your description of the position for which you are being interviewed?

19. Please tell me about yourself using words of only one syllable.

Closing Questions

20. Do you have any questions?

21. Well, based on what we have discussed, how do you feel about this job?

SCRIPT 2

Entry Level

Icebreaker and Background Questions

1. What did you learn from your internships/work study experiences?

2. What do you feel are the biggest challenges facing this field? This industry?

3. What aspects of your education/job do you rate as most critical?

Behavioral Questions

4. Tell me about a time when you were unable to complete a project on time.

5. Tell me about a time when you persuaded team members to do things your way.

6. Tell me about a time when you had to take an unpopular stand on a particular issue.

Questions to Determine Fit

7. What kinds of people do you prefer to work with?

8. What kinds of people do you find it difficult to work with?

Core Competency Questions

9. If you were to start college over again tomorrow, what courses would you take? Why?

10. Why don't I see internships or work study experiences on your résumé?

11. In college, how did you go about influencing someone to accept your ideas?

12. Based on what you know of the job market, which of your courses were the most useful? The least?

13. What advice would you give to a student starting college intending to go into your field?

Ethics Questions

14. What facts do you need in order to evaluate whether a proposed business decision is ethical?

15. What are some of the ethical implications of criticizing the job performance of a subordinate?

Brainteasers and Business Problems

16. Tell me about a time when your employer was not happy with your job performance.

17. Different is not always better, but better is always different. Can you describe something you have done that was new and different for your company and that improved performance and/or productivity?

Closing Questions

18. Do you have any questions?

19. Is there anything else I should know about you?

SCRIPT 3

Entry Level

Icebreaker and Background Questions

1. How do you know about this job and organization?

2. What kind of work do you want to do?

3. Tell me about your last/present job.

4. What do you think it takes for a person to be successful in your particular area?

Behavioral Questions

5. Tell me about a time when you wrote a program/report/strategic plan that was well received.

6. Tell me about a time when you anticipated potential problems and developed a proactive response.

7. Tell me about a time when you had to make an important decision with limited facts.

8. Tell me about a time when you said no to someone who asked you to drop everything to help him or her.

9. Tell me about a time when a team fell apart. Why did it happen, and what did you learn?

Questions to Determine Fit

10. What would your greatest business *champion* say about you?

11. What is the most important feature to you in a job?

12. Please rank the following from most important to least: (1) job duties, (2) hours, (3) distance from home to work, (4) pay, and (5) work environment.

13. What would your greatest business *adversary* say about you?

Core Competency Questions

14. In what courses did you get your worst grades? Why? How do you think that will affect your performance on the job?

15. Why did you decide to go to college?

16. Tell me about the most difficult sale you have had to make. What did you do to close the sale?

Ethics Questions

17. What are the warning signs that a proposed business decision may have ethical implications?

18. Can you describe a time when you were tempted to take an ethical shortcut but then reconsidered and took the high road?

Brainteasers and Business Problems

19. Who is the toughest employer you have ever had, and in what way was he or she the toughest?

20. Have you ever had to work with a manager who was unfair to you or who was just plain hard to work with? Please give details.

Closing Questions

21. Do you have any questions?

22. Is there any question that I should have asked you but did not?

SCRIPT 4

General

Icebreaker and Background Questions

1. How would your friends describe you? Your professors?

2. What else should I know about you?

3. How long have you been looking for a position?

4. What are your long-term goals?

5. How have previous jobs equipped you for greater responsibility?

Behavioral Questions

6. Tell me about a time when you were forced to make an unpopular decision.

7. Tell me about a time when you had to implement an unpopular decision.

8. Tell me about a time when you were tolerant of an opinion that was radically different from your own.

9. Tell me about a job or project for which you had to gather information from many different sources and then synthesize the information in support of a business challenge.

Questions to Determine Fit

10. What has been your greatest accomplishment in a work environment, and why do you consider it a great accomplishment?

11. How important are external deadlines in motivating you?

12. How do you feel about your present workload?

Core Competency Questions

13. Describe a time when you had to make an unpopular decision.

14. Tell me a little about some of your extracurricular activities that would assist you in this job.

15. Why are you working in a field other than the one in which you have a degree?

16. What have you done to stay current in your field?

Ethics Questions

17. What framework do you apply to test whether a proposed business decision is ethical?

18. What are the three most important ethical contributions you have made to a team or organization with which you have been associated?

Brainteasers and Business Problems

19. Do you agree with the statement that most people learn more from their mistakes than their successes? Why or why not?

20. How would you finish this sentence: Most people are basically . . . ?

Closing Questions

21. Do you have any questions?

SCRIPT 5

General

Icebreaker and Background Questions

1. What are your expectations of your future employer?

2. What two or three things are important to you in your new position?

3. What aspects of your current job would you consider to be crucial to the success of the business? Why?

4. What was the least relevant job you have held?

5. How long will it take for you to make a contribution?

Behavioral Questions

6. Tell me about a time when you were disappointed in your behavior.

7. Tell me about a time when you used your political savvy to push through a program you really believed in.

8. Tell me about a time when you had to deal with an irate customer.

Questions to Determine Fit

9. Give me an example of a situation in which you had to go above and beyond the call of duty to get something done.

10. What do you do when things are slow at work?

11. What have you learned from your mistakes?

12. How do you schedule and commit to quiet time?

13. How do you operate as a team player?

Core Competency Questions

14. Are you satisfied with the grades you received in school?

15. Do you think your grades accurately reflect your ability?

16. Have you ever received a grade lower than you expected? If so, what did you do about it?

17. Have you ever been put on the spot by a professor or advisor when you felt unsure of yourself? How did you handle it?

18. What competitive activities have you participated in? What did you learn from participation in competitive activities?

Ethics Questions

19. How do you define *business ethics*?

Brainteasers and Business Problems

20. Have you done your best work yet?

21. What cherished management belief have you had to give up in order to get where you are?

Closing Questions

22. Do you have any questions?

23. What implications have you drawn from the information you have learned today?

SCRIPT 6

General

Icebreaker and Background Questions

1. What goals have you set for yourself?

2. What did you enjoy most about your last/present job?

3. What did you enjoy least about your last/present job?

4. What can you do for us that someone else cannot?

Behavioral Questions

5. Tell me about a time when you delegated a project effectively.

6. Tell me about a time when you surmounted a major obstacle.

7. Tell me about a time when you set your sights too high.

8. If I were to interview your reporting staff members, how would they describe your strengths and weaknesses as a manager and supervisor?

Questions to Determine Fit

9. How do you deal with people whose backgrounds and value systems differ from yours?

10. Do you prefer working with others or working alone?

Core Competency Questions

11. Has competition had any positive or negative impact on your accomplishments? How?

12. What's one management lesson you learned in college?

13. Why do you want to get into this field?

14. What would you say to an interviewer who suggested that you do not have very much organizational work experience.

15. What qualities do you have that especially qualify you for this position?

16. Your résumé does not list any job experience in the past few years. Why not?

Ethics Questions

17. You are negotiating an important contract with another firm that has a reputation for driving a hard bargain. After a full day of negotiating, the other firm's representatives depart for the day. They leave behind a folder that appears to contain key information about their negotiating plans. What would you do?

18. How important is it for organizations to publish ethics policies and guidelines?

Brainteasers and Business Problems

19. What was the last product or service you saw that took your breath away?

20. What's the most significant compliment anyone has ever paid you?

Closing Questions

21. Do you have any questions?

22. Is there anything you'd like to know about the job that would help you to do it better than anyone else?

SCRIPT 7

Administration

Icebreaker and Background Questions

1. Who has had the greatest influence on the development of your career interests?

2. What were the biggest pressures on you in your last/present job?

Behavioral Questions

3. Tell me about a time when you went "out on a limb" in a job.

4. How do you like to be managed?

5. What good/bad work habits did you pick up from your first paying job?

6. Give me an example, from your past work experience, about a time when you had an underperforming employee reporting to you. How did you address the situation? Did the employee's performance improve? If not, what did you do next?

Questions to Determine Fit

7. How do you define *employee morale*?

8. What programs have you implemented to build morale among those reporting to you?

9. How do you keep your staff informed of new developments and organizational decisions?

10. Describe the relationship you feel should exist between a supervisor and those reporting to him or her.

Core Competency Questions

11. Under what conditions have you been most successful?

12. Tell me about a time when you had to pull a team together quickly.

13. How, specifically, do you contribute toward an environment of teamwork?

14. What can you do to promote a spirit of teamwork here?

15. What has been the employee turnover in your department over the past two years?

Ethics Questions

16. Can business ethics really be taught?

17. How does an organization best avoid punishing its employees for acting with ethical integrity and moral courage on their jobs when those actions might have a negative impact on the bottom line?

Brainteasers and Business Problems

18. Imagine I am blind. Describe blue to me.

19. Have you ever had a conflict at work that you couldn't resolve? How did you handle it?

Closing Questions

20. Do you have any questions?

21. If there were one reason why we should select you over the other applicants, what would that be?

SCRIPT 8

Administration

Icebreaker and Background Questions

1. How long have you been looking for a job?

2. How was your commute?

3. Are you familiar with our company?

Behavioral Questions

4. Tell me about a time when you set your sights too low.

5. Tell me about a time when you were able to convince others that you had a better way of doing things.

6. Rate your management skills on a scale of 1 to 10 with 10 representing excellent management skills. Provide three examples from your past work experiences that support your hierarchy.

Questions to Determine Fit

7. What two or three accomplishments have given you the most satisfaction? Why?

8. How can we best reward you for doing a good job?

9. Why do you want to leave your current position?

10. Why do you think you'll be successful in this job?

11. How do you know when a team has met its objectives?

12. Describe your approach to evaluating risk.

Core Competency Questions

13. Have you ever had to make an unpopular management decision? If so, tell me about it and how you handled it.

14. How do you go about assigning and scheduling projects and assignments?

15. Describe your leadership style for me.

16. How do you measure your success as a leader?

Ethics Questions

17. Is honesty *always* the best policy?

Brainteasers and Business Problems

18. How has your tolerance for accepting mistakes from your subordinates changed over the years?

19. What would your coworkers and subordinates say about your management style?

Closing Questions

20. Do you have any questions?

21. I've interviewed several very good candidates, and I will admit that you are one of them. What single message would you like me to remember that will convince me that *you* are the one we should hire?

SCRIPT 9

Administration

Icebreaker and Background Questions

1. How would you describe yourself?

2. Do you know much about our company/department/team?

3. Please take me through your professional career.

Behavioral Questions

4. Have you held other positions like the one you are applying for today? If yes, describe how you expect the positions to be similar.

5. In what ways do you expect your next job to differ from your last/present job?

6. What is the most important thing you have learned from your previous experience that you will bring to this job?

Questions to Determine Fit

7. Why have you chosen this particular field?

8. If we hire you, what are the top three goals you would like to see this company/department/team achieve?

9. What do you like most about this job?

10. How did you prepare for this interview?

Core Competency Questions

11. How do you determine which individuals need what training?

12. What training have you offered other people? How do you measure its impact?

13. If you are hired for this job, how will you approach the first 30 days?

14. What is the value of strategic planning to this job?

15. What intellectual challenge are you looking for in a job, and why?

Ethics Questions

16. How do you evaluate a business decision in terms of business ethics?

Brainteasers and Business Problems

17. You want to go swimming in a pool. The water is a little colder than comfortable. Are you the type of person who jumps in or the type who wades in?

18. Where do you think the power comes from in your organization? Why?

Closing Questions

19. Do you have any questions for us?

20. What have you observed so far about our firm and the interviewers you've met?

SCRIPT 10

Administration

Icebreaker and Background Questions

1. Can you name three things about this company that make you want to work here?

2. What are three words that describe you?

3. Would your supervisor be surprised to learn that you are seeking new employment?

4. How far can you advance with your current employer?

Behavioral Questions

5. If there were two things you could change in your last/present job, what would they be, and how would you change them?

6. Why did you leave your last job? (Or, why do you want to leave your present job?)

7. Describe the work environment or culture and its management style in which you have experienced the most success.

Questions to Determine Fit

8. Why do you think you were successful in your last job?

9. Can you recall a time when you were less than pleased with your performance?

10. Can you describe some projects that were a result of your own initiative?

11. What has prompted you in past jobs to initiate certain projects? How did the projects end up?

12. Have you been in charge of budgeting, approving expenses, and monitoring departmental progress against financial goals?

13. What would you consider to be the three most significant accomplishments in your business life?

Core Competency Questions

14. What do you do when you know you're right and others disagree with you?

15. Finish this sentence: Successful managers should . . .

16. What are the advantages of diversity in the workplace?

17. What does the term *time compression* mean to you?

18. What does the term *total quality management* mean to you?

19. Other than money (which is a given), what do you believe motivates people?

Ethics Questions

20. What's the unwritten ethical contract between you and the people that report to you?

Brainteasers and Business Problems

21. Do you agree with the statement that most people learn more from their mistakes than their successes? Why or why not?

22. If you had to eliminate one of the 50 states in the United States, which one would you eliminate and why?

Closing Questions

23. Do you have any questions?

SCRIPT 11

Administration

Icebreaker and Background Questions

1. How does this job compare with others you've applied for?

2. What important trends do you see in our industry?

3. In your last/present position, what features did/do you like the most? The least?

Behavioral Questions

4. Tell me about a time when you had a reporting employee who performed very well. The employee exceeded goals and sought more responsibility. Describe how you handled this situation day to day and over time.

5. How has your last/present job changed since you've held it?

6. Please describe your last/present supervisor's management style.

7. If you could make one constructive suggestion to your last/present CEO, what would it be?

Questions to Determine Fit

8. What suggestions did you make in your last job to improve outcomes such as suggestions to cut costs, increase profits, improve morale, or increase output?

9. What results did you get at your last/present job? How do you know? How did you measure results?

10. What would you like to have done more of in your last job?

11. What specific strengths did you bring to your last job?

Core Competency Questions

12. Can you give me three elements of your personal code of ethics for the workplace?

13. What experiences do you have in your background that show you are capable of creative risk taking?

14. What were your most memorable accomplishments in your last job?

15. Did you inaugurate any new policies/systems in any of the positions you've held?

16. What is the most difficult problem you have ever tackled? How did you approach the problem?

Ethics Questions

17. Do you think people in business behave less or more ethically today than they did 10 years ago? How has your own behavior changed during this time?

18. Tell me about a time when, by your actions, you made a lasting, positive impact on the ethical culture of your organization.

Brainteasers and Business Problems

19. If you could organize the world in one of three ways—no scarcity, no problems, or no rules—which way would you do it?

20. Which individual has been a major influence in your life?

Closing Questions

21. Do you have any questions?

SCRIPT 12

Administration

Icebreaker and Background Questions

1. Based on what you know about our industry right now, how does your ideal job stack up against the description of the job you're applying for?

Behavioral Questions

2. Can you give a ratio to express the amount of time you have worked alone to the amount of time you have worked with others?

3. How effectively did your boss handle evaluations?

4. Tell me about a method you've developed to accomplish a job. What were its strengths and weaknesses?

5. Tell me about a time when you had to make a decision that you knew would be unpopular.

6. Tell me about a time when you motivated a team in a unique way.

Questions to Determine Fit

7. What aspect of this job is the least appealing?

8. How do you plan your time?

9. What are three reasons for your success?

Core Competency Questions

10. How do you manage through delegating?

11. What does the term *global competition* mean to you?

12. Tell me what you think would be some good approaches to developing overseas markets during the next three years, especially considering the state of the dollar in today's international markets.

Ethics Questions

13. Your supervisor tells you to do something in a manner you are convinced is dead wrong. What would you do?

Brainteasers and Business Problems

14. How have you been an agent for change in your last/present position?

15. What is the worst thing you have heard about our company?

Closing Questions

16. Do you have any questions for us?

SCRIPT 13

Financial

Icebreaker and Background Questions

1. What two adjectives best describe you?

2. What would you say are some of the basic factors that motivate you in your work?

Behavioral Questions

3. Describe three components of your philosophy of management that demonstrate what you value and how those values enable you to add, as an individual, to an organization's culture and work environment.

4. Think back to a time when you trained a new employee. Tell me exactly what you did to train that employee and bring the person up to the job's performance standards.

5. Describe one of the best ideas you have ever sold to a peer or supervisor. What was your approach and result?

Questions to Determine Fit

6. Which is more important to you: the salary or the challenge?

7. What do you think determines a person's success in a firm?

8. Which coworker at your last job did you get along with least well? What did you do about it?

Core Competency Questions

9. I see you managed the payroll for three subsidiaries. What was the most difficult part of integrating all of them?

10. Describe the most significant internal control weaknesses you have ever identified and what you did to remedy them. What were the results?

11. Describe the most significant accounting operations reengineering project you have led. What were the results?

12. Do you perform employee salary reviews? If yes, what is your approach?

13. Tell me how you go about creating an annual budget.

14. What problems do you have in staying within your budget?

Ethics Questions

15. Have you ever spent time at work on personal projects? What would you do to an employee who did this?

Brainteasers and Business Problems

16. What do you want to hear first, the good news or the bad news?

17. Think back over the past two or three years and recall a work situation that stands out in your mind as a turning point. Describe what it was, who was involved, what your role was, and what the outcome was.

Closing Questions

18. Do you have any questions for us?

SCRIPT 14

Financial

Icebreaker and Background Questions

1. If you could make a wish, what would be your perfect job?

Behavioral Questions

2. Tell me about a time your knowledge of financial and business operations made a difference in the company's profits.

Questions to Determine Fit

3. What experience do you have that qualifies you for this job?

4. How do you think your supervisor will react when you tender your resignation?

5. Describe the most significant report or presentation you have had to prepare.

6. What idea have you developed and implemented that was particularly creative or innovative?

Core Competency Questions

7. When you were the marketing manager for _____, what steps did you take in planning the annual marketing budget?

8. How do you manage others day to day while focusing on the big picture?

9. Distinguish between planning for the short term, midterm, and long term.

10. How do you quantify the results of your activities as a manager?

11. Have you ever completed a formal return-on-investment calculation on a strategic investment? Please provide details.

Ethics Questions

12. You discover that a recently hired colleague is earning much more in salary than you earn. What do you do?

Brainteasers and Business Problems

13. If your photograph were splashed on a magazine cover, what would the magazine be, and what would the headline say?

14. How would you rate me as an interviewer?

Closing Questions

15. Do you have any questions for us?

SCRIPT 15

Financial

Icebreaker and Background Questions

1. What would your last boss tell me about you?

2. Why do you want to work for us?

Behavioral Questions

3. What were the biggest decisions you made in the past six months?

4. How have you gone about making major decisions in the past six months, and what alternatives did you consider?

5. Can you describe a major project with which you encountered problems?

6. How have you resolved problems you have encountered on major projects, and what were the results?

7. What factors are crucial within an organization and must be present for you to work most effectively?

Questions to Determine Fit

8. Why do you think you are a good match for this job?

9. What goals have you set for yourself in your career?

10. How do you see our company helping you achieve your goals?

Core Competency Questions

11. How do you deal with unanticipated expenses? Can you give an example?

12. How do you defend the budget in your present position?

13. Tell me about a time when you underestimated a budget and had to ask for additional funds.

14. Did you ever have to restructure your budget in the middle of the fiscal period? What approach did you take?

15. How would you create a budget in the position for which you are applying?

16. What process do you use for evaluating the training and developmental needs of subordinates?

Ethics Questions

17. Describe your previous employer's strategy for managing ethics.

Brainteasers and Business Problems

18. How have you benefited from your disappointments?

19. Can you suggest three reasons why manhole covers are circular?

Closing Questions

20. Do you have any questions for us?

SCRIPT 16

General Management and/or Supervision

Icebreaker and Background Questions

1. Can you tell me a little about yourself?

2. Describe a great day at the job of your dreams.

Behavioral Questions

3. Tell me about a time when you reorganized a department or significantly changed employee work assignments. How did you approach the task? How did the affected employees respond to your actions?

4. What strategies have you devised to handle employees' resistance to change?

5. How do you know you are doing a good job?

6. How do you prefer to measure performance?

7. Tell me about a time when you had to react quickly to a rapidly evolving situation.

8. Can you give me an example of a situation you have handled which would demonstrate your ability to supervise?

Questions to Determine Fit

9. What kinds of obstacles to completing assignments on time do you most frequently encounter at work?

10. If you have complaints about your present company and you believe they think highly of you, why haven't you brought your concerns to their attention?

11. The successful candidate for this position will be working with some highly trained individuals who have been with the company for a long time. How will you fit in with them?

12. What is the most difficult situation you have faced? How did you handle it?

13. What can you bring to this job from your previous experience?

14. What do you like the best about supervision?

15. What do you like the least about supervision?

16. What has been your most positive experience as a supervisor?

17. What has been your most negative experience as a supervisor?

18. Which aspect of supervision did you feel the most comfortable with?

19. Which aspect of supervision did you feel the least comfortable with?

20. What aspect of supervision is most difficult for you, and why?

Core Competency Questions

21. What's the hardest thing about being a leader?

22. Are you a mentor to anyone? Who? What is your philosophy of mentoring?

23. What does the word *success* mean to you?

24. What does the word *failure* mean to you?

25. What experience have you had in supervision?

26. What experience have you had in resolving grievances?

27. What experience have you had in investigating discrimination and/or sexual harassment complaints?

28. Have you had any experience in applying the provisions of the Americans with Disabilities Act?

29. Under which circumstances would you refer an employee to the employee assistance program?

Ethics Questions

30. What do you think about the *balanced-scorecard approach* to corporate social responsibility?

Brainteasers and Business Problems

31. Describe a situation in which your work or ideas were criticized.

32. You supervise a group of employees. One employee complains that the office is too hot, another employee complains that the office is too cold. How would you handle this?

33. What is the role of a supervisor?

Closing Questions

34. Do you have any questions for us?

SCRIPT 17

General Management and/or Supervision

Icebreaker and Background Questions

1. Can you tell me a little about yourself?

Behavioral Questions

2. A manager or supervisor must manage performance and conduct periodic performance reviews. Tell me how you have managed employee performance in the past. Describe the process you have used to give performance feedback.

3. Tell me about a difficult decision you have had to make.

4. With respect to a time when you had to make a difficult decision, what did you learn from that experience?

5. Describe the way your department is currently organized.

Questions to Determine Fit

6. What kind of leader are you? Please provide an example.

7. What is the title of the person you report to, and what are his or her responsibilities?

8. What would your boss say about your performance in your last position?

9. What qualifications do you have to make you successful in this field?

10. Do you prefer to speak with someone or send him or her a memo?

Core Competency Questions

11. Describe a problem that you solved using employee involvement.

12. Tell me about an employee who became more successful as a result of your management.

13. Describe your system for controlling errors in your own work and the work of your staff.

14. Tell me about the most difficult employee situation you have ever had to handle. What did you do about it, and what was the result?

Ethics Questions

15. Who should be responsible for ethics in the company?

Brainteasers and Business Problems

16. Which management gurus do you find most interesting?

17. When you've had a really good day at work and you go home and kick back and you feel satisfied, what was it about that day that made you feel really good?

18. When you have had a really bad day at work and you go home and feel upset, what was it about that day that made you feel really upset?

Closing Questions

19. Do you have any questions for us?

20. What do you want to be doing five years from now?

SCRIPT 18

General Management and/or Supervision

Icebreaker and Background Questions

1. Can you tell me a little about yourself?

2. What books and/or magazines do you read?

3. I've read your résumé and application, but what else should I know about you to make a good decision about your qualifications for this job?

Behavioral Questions

4. Tell me about a time when your knowledge of your position made a difference in the outcome of a situation.

5. Can you describe a situation in which a crisis occurred and you had to shift priorities and workload quickly?

6. How do you feel about your present workload?

Questions to Determine Fit

7. Have you thought about why you might prefer to work with our firm as opposed to one of the other firms at which you've applied?

8. When some managers make a decision, they often feel a need to defend it at any cost or despite new information. Can you describe a

time when you changed a stated decision or opinion because you were persuaded you were wrong?

9. What skill has been praised or rewarded in your past positions?

10. What would you do differently in your life? Your career?

Core Competency Questions

11. What are your most important long-term goals?

12. Describe the people that you hired on your last job. How long did they last, and how did they work out?

13. What has been your experience with major expansion or reduction of force?

14. How many immediate subordinates have you selected in the past two years? How did you go about it? Any surprises or disappointments?

15. How many immediate subordinates have you removed from their jobs in the last few years?

Ethics Questions

16. What is the first step to ensuring that people in the firm be equipped to recognize and resolve moral dilemmas?

Brainteasers and Business Problems

17. How has your perspective of quality evolved over your career?

18. How has your tolerance for accepting mistakes from your subordinates changed over the years?

19. What is the most satisfying business compliment that you have ever been paid?

Closing Questions

20. Do you have any questions for us?

SCRIPT 19

General Management and/or Supervision

Icebreaker and Background Questions

1. Can you tell me a little about yourself?

2. What sort of position are you really looking for? Can you describe your ideal job?

Behavioral Questions

3. Some people feel that spending a prolonged time at one job demonstrates a lack of initiative. How do you respond to that?

4. What are the advantages of staying at one job for a long time?

5. Tell me about a time when you solved a problem in a unique manner.

6. Give me an example of a time when you used your strengths to achieve outstanding results.

Questions to Determine Fit

7. Since you were in the same job for such a long time, you've probably grown very comfortable in it—maybe even a bit stale. How would you cope with a new job in a company such as ours?

Core Competency Questions

8. Would your subordinates describe you as a delegator, and why would they describe you that way?

9. Some managers keep a very close check on their organizations. Others use a loose rein. What level of control do you prefer? How has it changed in the last few years?

10. What have been the most important surprises you have received from a particular situation's getting out of control? Why did the situation get out of control?

11. Let's talk about standards of performance. How would you describe your own standards? What would your subordinates say? What would your boss say?

12. Sometimes it is necessary to issue an edict to an individual or to the entire staff. Do you have any recent examples of edicts you have issued?

Ethics Questions

13. In general, are people in organizations provided with a safe opportunity to discuss ethical issues of concern? What are some ways to promote such safe opportunities?

Brainteasers and Business Problems

14. What makes you unique?

15. What would you like to see inscribed on your headstone?

16. On what occasions are you tempted to lie?

Closing Questions

17. Do you have any questions for us?

SCRIPT 20

General Management and/or Supervision

Icebreaker and Background Questions

1. Can you tell me a little about yourself?

2. Where do you want to be—and what do you want to be doing—five years from now?

Behavioral Questions

3. When you have entered a new workplace in the past, as a manager or supervisor, describe how you have gone about meeting and developing relationships with your new coworkers, supervisors, and reporting staff.

4. Tell me about a time when you used creativity in your last/present position.

Questions to Determine Fit

5. What experiences do you bring that involve creativity?

6. How important is it for you to learn new skills?

7. What new skills would you like to learn?

8. Do you consider yourself successful?

Core Competency Questions

9. What specific behaviors do you think contribute to your effectiveness as a supervisor?

10. What specific behaviors do you think might interfere with your effectiveness as a supervisor?

11. In what respects do you feel you have improved most as a supervisor during the last few years?

12. Some managers are quite deliberate about such things as communications, development, and motivation. Do you have examples of how you have addressed these areas?

13. How would you characterize your relationships with your last three supervisors? Any patterns?

14. This position requires a lot of outside-of-the-box thinking. How comfortable are you with thinking creatively?

Ethics Questions

15. You determine that a problem employee must be dismissed. Do you provide minimum or maximum notice to the employee? Why?

Brainteasers and Business Problems

16. The business world is full of euphemisms. What's your current favorite?

17. Should all business relationships have fixed terms—that is, expiration dates?

Closing Questions

18. Do you have any questions for us?

SCRIPT 21

General Management and/or Supervision

Icebreaker and Background Questions

1. Can you tell me a little about yourself?

Behavioral Questions

2. Tell me about a time when your communication style made a difference in a project.

3. As a manager or supervisor, one of your jobs is to provide direction and leadership for a work unit. Describe how you have accomplished this in the past.

4. Tell me about a situation in which you were able to find a new and better way of doing something significant.

5. Give me an example that would show that you've been able to develop and maintain productive relations with others, though there were differing points of view.

Questions to Determine Fit

6. How would you describe your communication style?

Core Competency Questions

7. Some managers are short-fused and impatient in their reactions. How would you describe yourself in these dimensions?

8. Most of us can look back on new ideas, new projects, or innovations we feel proud that we introduced. Would you describe one or two such innovations you are particularly proud of?

9. What are the legitimate uses for office gossip or the rumor mill?

10. How would you handle a subordinate who deliberately went about a task in a way that contradicted your instructions yet was wildly successful?

11. Are you prepared to fill in for someone who has different, even lower-level, responsibilities?

Ethics Questions

12. Your boss is going on vacation for a month. Although it isn't in your job description to do so, she asks you to work for another manager in her absence. What would you say and do?

13. How do you differentiate between fairness and justice?

Brainteasers and Business Problems

14. Is there anything positive to be said about conventional wisdom?

15. Describe a time when you unfairly got caught up in office politics.

16. What is the difference between management and leadership?

Closing Questions

17. Do you have any questions for us?

SCRIPT 22

Team Leadership

Icebreaker and Background Questions

1. Can you tell me a little about yourself?

2. Who or what has been a major influence in your life?

Behavioral Questions

3. Tell me about a time when your team made emotional decisions about a particular project. What happened, and how did you handle it?

4. Tell me about a specific accomplishment you have achieved as a participant in a team.

Questions to Determine Fit

5. What are your strengths? What are your weaknesses?

6. Can you give me an example of a time when you received constructive criticism?

7. What makes you want to work hard?

8. What past accomplishments gave you satisfaction?

9. What type of work environment do you like best?

10. Explain how you overcame a major obstacle.

11. How do you handle pressure and stress?

Core Competency Questions

12. What is one thing a teammate can say to you that is guaranteed to make you lose confidence in him or her?

13. How do you get along with superiors?

14. How do you get along with coworkers?

15. How do you get along with people you've supervised?

16. What are your team-player qualities? Please be specific.

Ethics Questions

17. What is your opinion about professional success that results from pursuing well-thought-out plans versus success that comes from taking advantage of unanticipated opportunities? Why?

Brainteasers and Business Problems

18. What's the difference between a manager and a leader?

Closing Questions

19. Do you have any questions for us?

SCRIPT 23

Team Leadership

Icebreaker and Background Questions

1. Can you tell me a little about yourself?

2. What are some of your pet peeves?

3. How would you describe your organizational style?

Behavioral Questions

4. Tell me about a time when you had to confront a team member.

5. Tell me about a time when you initiated an action that brought unexpected results.

6. Can you describe a time when your performance exceeded expectations?

7. Tell me about an unsuccessful team of which you were a member. What, if anything, could you have done differently?

8. Tell me about a successful team of which you were a member. What was the most outstanding characteristic of that team? What specifically did you contribute?

Questions to Determine Fit

9. As a member of a team, how do you see your role?

10. If you were a team leader and a team member wanted to do something in a way you were convinced was a mistake, what would you do?

11. Give me an example of your working with diverse groups of people, including those with less experience.

12. What are the important qualities a person should have in order to become an effective team member?

13. What qualities do you have that make you an effective team player?

14. As a leader, what attributes do you look for in team members?

15. What can you contribute to establish a positive working environment for our team?

16. What type of people do you work best with?

Core Competency Questions

17. As a member of a team, how do you handle a team member who is not pulling his or her weight?

18. Have you ever been on a team in which people overruled you or wouldn't let you get a word in edgewise? How did you handle it?

19. Tell us about your experience in migrating from one application to another. What steps did you take to maintain user satisfaction during the migration?

Ethics Questions

20. Which organization in your life has earned your deepest sense of loyalty? What ties you to that organization's principles and activities?

Brainteasers and Business Problems

21. What are the characteristics of a successful team?

22. What's more important to you, truth or comfort?

23. How would you react if I told you that your interview, so far, was *terrible*?

Closing Questions

24. Do you have any questions for us?

SCRIPT 24

Team Leadership

Icebreaker and Background Questions

1. Can you tell me a little about yourself?

2. What are the reasons for your success?

Behavioral Questions

3. Tell me about a time when you had to handle a personnel problem and what you did.

4. Think of something that you consider a failure in your career. What did you learn from it?

Questions to Determine Fit

5. You say that one of your strengths is follow-through. When has that made a difference in your work?

6. Of all the work you have done, where have you been the most successful?

7. Describe how your job relates to the overall goals of your department and company.

8. What are the most repetitive tasks in your job?

Core Competency Questions

9. What have you learned about guarding against groupthink?

10. Have you developed any special techniques for brainstorming?

11. Are you able to predict a person's behavior based on your reading of him or her?

12. Describe your organizational skills.

13. What strategies do you apply to working with disorganized colleagues?

14. Have you ever not taken a risk and later regretted it?

15. Tell me about an occasion when the team objected to your ideas. What did you do to persuade them of your point of view?

16. What factors would you consider in assembling a project team?

17. Name some of the pitfalls to be avoided in building an effective team.

18. Through what tools can a committee become more useful or productive?

19. What actions can a supervisor take to establish teamwork in the organization?

20. You supervise a group of civilian employees. Your employees appear to be at odds with the uniformed personnel. What steps can you take to improve the teamwork between civilian and uniformed personnel?

21. What are the advantages, if any, of establishing team goals as opposed to individual goals?

Ethics Questions

22. If you knew that millions of people would model their lives after yours, would you change anything about the way you live? When have you changed your behavior to try to influence someone else?

Brainteasers and Business Problems

23. When is it better to ask for forgiveness than to ask for permission?

24. Tell me about the most successful risk you've ever taken.

Closing Questions

25. Do you have any questions for us?

SCRIPT 25

Sales and Marketing and/or Sales Management

Icebreaker and Background Questions

1. Can you tell me a little about yourself?

Behavioral Questions

2. Tell me about a time when you almost lost a sale and worked hard to get it back.

3. When you cold-call a prospect, what obstacles do you expect the clerical staff to put in your way?

4. When you telephone a prospect, what strategies do you use to get past the secretary or receptionist?

Questions to Determine Fit

5. How do you qualify a prospect?

6. How do you overcome the difficult periods that face everyone in sales?

7. How long does it take you to get from initial contact to sales closing?

8. How do you deal with rejection?

Core Competency Questions

9. What strategies do you employ for finding common ground with your customers?

10. Have you found it helpful to take notes when talking to a customer?

11. If I were a prospect, what clues about me does this office tell you?

12. Can you give an example of how you are able to be positive about a product even when discussing a negative?

Ethics Questions

13. When you make a decision, are you generally more concerned about its immediate impact or its long-range consequences? How much have you changed in this regard during the past decade?

Brainteasers and Business Problems

14. Can you sell me on our product/service?

15. Which of your skills can stand improvement at this time?

Closing Questions

16. Do you have any questions for us?

SCRIPT 26

Sales and Marketing and/or Sales Management

Icebreaker and Background Questions

1. Can you tell me a little about yourself?

2. Can you think of a challenge you have faced? How did you deal with it?

Behavioral Questions

3. Tell me about a time you adjusted your approach to a prospect based on his or her body language.

4. Tell me about a time when you followed up with a reluctant prospect and still failed to get the order.

5. Talk about a time when you overcame your own mental block or prejudices to make a sale.

Questions to Determine Fit

6. What strategies do you use to repeat the customer's key concepts back to him or her during a sales pitch?

7. How do you turn an occasional buyer into a regular buyer?

8. Have you ever taken over an existing territory/desk? What was the volume when you started? What was it when you left?

Core Competency Questions

9. What have you learned about using sales incentives to promote sales?

10. What strategies do you use to plant questions in your customers' minds?

11. When is it appropriate to ask a prospect, "How much do you want to spend?"

Ethics Questions

12. When was the last time you did something solely to help the larger community beyond your family and friends? Do you think you have an obligation to serve the community?

Brainteasers and Business Problems

13. Are you the type of person that prefers to make lists or the type that prefers to strike items off lists?

14. Tell me about a boss you did not get along with.

Closing Questions

15. Do you have any questions for us?

16. What did you accomplish at work the day before yesterday—in detail?

SCRIPT 27

Sales and Marketing and/or Sales Management

Icebreaker and Background Questions

1. Can you tell me a little about yourself?

2. What makes you proud of your work?

Behavioral Questions

3. What was the most surprising objection you have ever received, and how did you handle it?

4. Can you talk about a sales incentive program that motivated you?

Questions to Determine Fit

5. What do you despise about making telephone sales calls?

6. Who are the motivation gurus you find most interesting?

Core Competency Questions

7. Where do you find your telephone leads?

8. What is your ratio of initial contacts to actual sales presentations?

9. What percentage of your sales calls result in sales?

10. What are the five most common objections you face, and how do you deal with them?

Ethics Questions

11. In what ways are your ethics in business different from your ethics in your personal life?

12. In what ways is the Golden Rule an insufficient model for a corporate ethics policy?

Brainteasers and Business Problems

13. Finish this sentence: I know I am taking a risk when . . .

14. What would be impossible for you to do, but if you could do it, would greatly increase your productivity, results, and/or success?

Closing Questions

15. Do you have any questions for us?

SCRIPT 28

Sales and Marketing and/or Sales Management

Icebreaker and Background Questions

1. Can you tell me a little about yourself?

2. Are you a self-starter? Can you give me an example of an instance in which you have taken the initiative?

Behavioral Questions

3. What is your definition of *sales*?

4. Can you tell me about a time when you identified a new, unusual, or different approach for addressing a problem or task?

5. Tell us about your experience in dealing with the public.

Questions to Determine Fit

6. How would you describe your assertiveness?

7. Who was the toughest customer you ever faced?

Core Competency Questions

8. When was the last time you sent a thank you note to a customer who didn't buy that day?

9. How do you try to show each customer that he or she is important?

10. This job requires a large amount of travel. How do you handle the stress of traveling?

11. How would you go about identifying customers in a new market?

12. What have you figured out about prospecting for customers or developing new markets in cyberspace?

Ethics Questions

13. Do you think you have a better reputation in your professional or personal dealings?

Brainteasers and Business Problems

14. What is your philosophy of mentoring?

Closing Questions

15. Do you have any questions for us?

SCRIPT 29

Customer Service

Icebreaker and Background Questions

1. Can you tell me a little about yourself?

2. We're all customers. What frustrates you about customer service?

Behavioral Questions

3. If you had a customer who was complaining about poor service, how would you handle it?

4. Tell me about your worst customer service dilemma and how you overcame it.

5. Can you tell me about a difficult collection problem and how you dealt with it?

Questions to Determine Fit

6. What's one thing we at this company could do to make our customers even more satisfied with us?

7. What is the customer service attitude at your present organization?

Core Competency Questions

8. How do you deal with customers who think they are right even when they are wrong?

9. At your last job, how often did you take a survey of customer satisfaction?

10. What strategies have you learned to encourage customers to pay on time?

11. What strategies have you developed to listen to emotional customers without getting hooked?

Ethics Questions

12. How do you define *integrity*? What is the relationship between individual integrity and business ethics?

Brainteasers and Business Problems

13. What is the most significant improvement in customer service that you have achieved in the last year?

14. How has technology made customer service better, and how has technology made it worse?

Closing Questions

15. Do you have any questions for us?

SCRIPT 30

Training and/or Presentation Skills

Icebreaker and Background Questions

1. Can you tell me a little about yourself?

2. What were the most important projects you worked on at your last/present job?

Behavioral Questions

3. Can you give me an example of a major project you have worked on that involved communication and writing skills?

4. Tell me about a work situation that required excellent communication skills.

5. Can you recall a time when you persuaded someone who initially disagreed with you to ultimately see the correctness of your position?

6. Give me an example of your using strategic thinking at work.

7. Tell me about a time when your communication style influenced a decision.

Questions to Determine Fit

8. How would you compare your oral skills to your writing skills?

9. What's one thing that should never be communicated in a memo or e-mail?

10. What are the most difficult aspects of your current job, and how do you approach them?

11. What has been your most important work-related innovation or contribution?

12. What has caused you the most problems in executing your tasks?

13. How do you organize and plan for major projects? Recall a major project you have worked on; how did you organize and plan for it?

Core Competency Questions

14. What experience have you had in making oral presentations? How do you rate your skills in this area?

15. When do you have trouble communicating with people?

16. When you are assigned to work with new people, how do you go about getting to know them—how they work and what their strengths and weaknesses are?

17. How often do you communicate with the person who receives the output of your work?

Ethics Questions

18. How do you balance the competing needs of shareholders, employees, customers, partners, and the community and/or environment?

Brainteasers and Business Problems

19. If you had the opportunity to do the last 10 years of your career over again, what would you do differently?

20. An employee continues to make careless mistakes. How will you address the situation?

Closing Questions

21. Do you have any questions for us?

SCRIPT 31

Project Management

Icebreaker and Background Questions

1. Can you tell me a little about yourself?

Behavioral Questions

2. Can you think of a time when you disagreed with your supervisor on a tactical matter?

3. Tell me about a time when, rather than following instructions, you went about a task in your own way.

4. Tell me about a team project of which you are particularly proud. What was your specific contribution?

Questions to Determine Fit

5. What do you do to make the people around you feel important, appreciated, and respected?

6. What organizations do you see as this company's chief competition? Can you compare and contrast the organizations?

7. Can you think of an example of something you have learned from someone else's mistake?

8. What risks did you take in your last few jobs? What was the result of your taking those risks?

Core Competency Questions

9. What are some examples of important types of decisions or recommendations you have been called upon to make?

10. Would you describe how you have approached making important decisions or recommendations? With whom did you consult?

11. Tell me what you have learned about reducing employee turnover.

12. How do you prioritize your time?

13. Take me through a project on which you demonstrated _____ skills.

Ethics Questions

14. How do you include business ethics into the mix when recruiting?

Brainteasers and Business Problems

15. Describe the most difficult decision you have ever had to make. Reflecting back, was your decision the best possible choice you could have made? Why or why not?

16. How successful do you believe you've been so far?

Closing Questions

17. Do you have any questions for us?

SCRIPT 32

Project Management

Icebreaker and Background Questions

1. Can you tell me a little about yourself?

Behavioral Questions

2. What would you do if your priorities conflicted with the priorities of a colleague also on the project?

3. Tell me about a complex problem you have had to deal with.

4. Tell me about a time when it was your job to negotiate a deal.

5. Tell me about a time when you solved a difficult problem at work.

6. Tell me about a time when you failed to reach a goal.

7. Think of a crisis situation that got out of control. Why did it happen, and what was your role in the chain of events?

Questions to Determine Fit

8. What decisions are easiest for you to make, and which ones are more difficult?

9. Are you required to analyze data at your current job?

10. Most of us can think of an important decision that we would make quite differently if we were to make it again. Can you cite any examples of such decisions from your own experience?

Core Competency Questions

11. What is your process for setting priorities?

12. How do you approach long-term projects?

13. How would you describe your problem-solving ability?

14. Most of us become more astute decision makers as the base of our experience broadens. In what respects do you feel you have improved as a decision maker?

15. Describe a situation that required you to use fact-finding skills.

16. How many projects can you handle at a time?

Ethics Questions

17. If two managers give you two projects to be completed by the end of the day and you have time to do only one, how do you proceed?

Brainteasers and Business Problems

18. In your career, what negotiation are you most proud of?

19. What has been your biggest analytical challenge?

Closing Questions

20. Do you have any questions for us?

SCRIPT 33

Project Management

Icebreaker and Background Questions

1. Can you tell me a little about yourself?

Behavioral Questions

2. Tell me about a time when you lost/won an important contract or sale.

3. Can you tell me about a specific situation in which you prevented a problem before it occurred?

4. Give me an example of a time when management had to change a plan or approach to which you were committed. How did you feel, and how did you explain the change to your team?

5. Tell me about a job or project for which you had to gather information from many different sources and then create something with the information.

6. Tell me about a time when you had to make a big personal adaptation to get the work done.

Questions to Determine Fit

7. I'm interested in how you accomplish project planning. What planning processes have you found useful, and how do you go about implementing them?

8. What is your management style?

9. Are you a good manager? Can you give me some examples of successes you have had as a manager? Do you feel that you have top managerial potential?

10. What do you look for when you hire people?

11. Have you ever had to fire people? What were the reasons, and how did you handle the situation?

12. What do you think is the most difficult thing about being a manager or executive?

Core Competency Questions

13. Prioritize the elements of a complicated project.

14. Do you use an activity chart to track the flow of the activities necessary to reach your goals?

15. What project management methodologies have you found most effective?

16. In what ways have you improved in your capacity for planning over the years?

17. What do you do when there is a decision to be made and no procedure exists?

Ethics Questions

18. How might you be able to gauge a person's ethical mindset in an interview?

Brainteasers and Business Problems

19. Tell me about a time when you had a conflict in your work and how you resolved it.

20. How would you describe your management philosophy?

21. If you could eliminate one responsibility from your last job, what would it be?

Closing Questions

22. Do you have any questions for us?

SCRIPT 34

Human Resources Management

Icebreaker and Background Questions

1. Can you tell me a little about yourself?

2. What are the most important rewards you expect out of your career?

Behavioral Questions

3. Give me an example of a time when you were assertive and took the initiative to get a particular job done.

4. Tell me about how you would budget for recruiting.

5. Tell me about a time when you hired/fired the wrong person.

Questions to Determine Fit

6. If you were hiring someone for the job you are interviewing for, what three qualities would you look for?

7. Do you have a favorite interviewing question you like to ask candidates?

8. What do you do to welcome and orient new hires into your department or team?

Core Competency Questions

9. How do you handle personnel evaluations?

10. What's the first thing you look for on a résumé or application?

11. How do you go about checking references?

12. What questions would you ask, or techniques would you use, to establish if a particular person were willing to do the job?

13. How many people have you hired in the past two years? Into what positions?

14. What has your experience been with retaining recruitment firms?

15. What strategies have you developed for handling counteroffers?

Ethics Questions

16. There are two applicants for one job. They have identical qualifications in every respect. How do you decide?

Brainteasers and Business Problems

17. If you were going to be fired, how would you like your supervisor to handle it?

18. What would you do if everyone in your department called in sick at the same time?

Closing Questions

19. Do you have any questions for us?

SCRIPT 35

Human Resources Management

Icebreaker and Background Questions

1. Can you tell me a little about yourself?

2. Tell me about a project that got you really excited.

Behavioral Questions

3. Tell me about a time when you had to assert yourself in a difficult situation.

4. Tell me about your biggest hiring success.

5. Tell me about your biggest hiring mistake.

Questions to Determine Fit

6. To what do you attribute turnover?

7. Is turnover always detrimental?

8. Tell me about a time when you had to discipline a subordinate.

Core Competency Questions

9. Is any level of employee turnover acceptable?

10. How could we improve the hiring process we are using to select a person for this position?

11. What programs have you found to be successful in retaining employees?

12. What are the typical problems and grievances that your staff brings to you? How do you handle them?

13. How do you maintain discipline within your department or team?

14. What is the most common cause of termination in your experience?

15. Have you thought about violence in the workplace? What strategies have you developed to address this issue?

Ethics Questions

16. Why should companies or employees worry about doing things ethically?

Brainteasers and Business Problems

17. What is your concept of workplace discipline?

18. If your last boss were able to wave a magic wand over your head, what aspect of your performance would he or she fine-tune?

Closing Questions

19. Do you have any questions for us?

SCRIPT 36

Information Technology Management, Java Expertise

Icebreaker and Background Questions

1. Can you tell me a little about yourself?

2. What kind of supervisor is likely to get the best performance out of you?

Behavioral Questions

3. Describe a situation in which you were able to enhance the usefulness of information in an existing mainframe system and increase your employer's productivity.

4. Tell me about a time when you were required to work with people you had not previously worked with.

5. What would you do if you had almost completed a project and the specifications changed?

6. Tell me about a recent and relevant project experience in which you brought together a team to interpret functional specifications and translated that into a sound technical project.

7. How has your conception of information systems quality evolved over the years?

8. Describe successful strategies for software testing that you have employed.

Questions to Determine Fit

9. When have you had to adapt in your work?

10. How would you describe your ability to work with others?

11. Give me some examples of different approaches you have used when persuading someone to cooperate with you.

12. How do you cope with the inevitable stresses and pressures of your job?

13. How do you keep abreast of new developments in information technology?

Core Competency Questions

14. I see that you program in [whatever language]. How would you link an indexed field variable to display on mouseover?

15. How do you test your code?

16. Given a simple program designed to take inputs of integers from 1 to 1,000 and to output the factorial value of that number, how would you test this program? You do not have access to the code. Please be as specific as possible.

17. What is the difference between an *interface* and an *abstract class*?

18. What is the purpose of garbage collection in Java, and when is it used?

19. Have you seen our advertising? Our commercials or corporate branding spots? What seemed to you to be effective about them? How would you make them more effective?

Ethics Questions

20. How important is it to have a values statement? What should the values statement include?

Brainteasers and Business Problems

21. What has been the most useful technical criticism you have ever received?

22. What would be impossible for you to do, but if you could do it, it would greatly increase your productivity, results, and/or success?

Closing Questions

23. Do you have any questions for us?

SCRIPT 37

Information Technology Management, Database Administration Expertise

Icebreaker and Background Questions

1. Can you tell me a little about yourself?

Behavioral Questions

2. Describe the most significant business process reengineering project you have led. What were the results?

3. Describe the central attributes of the object paradigm. How does encapsulation or polymorphism contribute to the technology's effectiveness?

4. Tell me about a time when you had to meet multiple deadlines in a short period. How were you able to accomplish this?

5. Tell me about a time you were unable to meet an important deadline. How did you handle this problem?

6. Please describe the most difficult task you have ever had to perform using a specific tool, and describe how you managed to accomplish it.

Questions to Determine Fit

7. What are the biggest challenges you face when you are required to work with others?

8. Have your team members ever come to you with their personal problems? What limits, if any, have you put on those interactions?

9. What plan of action do you take when facing a problem?

10. What is the most boring project you have ever worked on? How did you do on it?

11. How do you react to criticism from superiors if you believe it is unwarranted?

12. Describe the best company you have ever worked for.

Core Competency Questions

13. What metrics do you prefer to measure user satisfaction with IT?

14. Have you seen or used our product(s) or service(s)? What did you like or not like about them?

15. What is *blocking*, and how would you troubleshoot it?

16. What is a *deadlock*, and what is a *livelock*? How will you go about resolving deadlocks?

17. Describe synchronization with respect to multithreading.

18. What is an *abstract class*?

19. Explain different ways of using thread.

20. What are *statistics*? Under what circumstances do they go out of date? How do you update them?

21. What are *cursors*? Explain different types of cursors. What are the disadvantages of cursors? How can you avoid cursors?

22. What are *joins*? Explain the different types of joins.

23. Describe the project or situation that best demonstrates your coding skills.

24. Describe the project or situation that best demonstrates your analytical abilities.

25. Give me an example of an idea that you developed, and describe how you "sold" it within the organization.

26. What is *normalization*? Explain different levels of normalization.

27. Can you give me an example of a skill that you learned on your own—that is, a skill you did not learn in the context of a formal classroom environment?

28. What have you invented during the past five years?

29. Explain different isolation levels.

30. What are *constraints*? Explain different types of constraints.

31. What are the elements included in strategic planning?

Ethics Questions

32. Can you give an example of a situation in which an employee's actions might not be ethical but are not against the law either? How would you advise the employee?

Brainteasers and Business Problems

33. Design a bathroom for Bill Gates.

34. How would you reinvent our business from an IT perspective if you had a blank sheet of paper and no resource constraints?

Closing Questions

35. Do you have any questions for us?

SCRIPT 38

Information Technology Management, Network Administration Expertise

Icebreaker and Background Questions

1. Can you tell me a little about yourself?

Behavioral Questions

2. Tell me about a time you were required to make a decision that could have had negative outcomes. How did you make this decision?

3. Tell me about a time when you made a suboptimum decision about a project.

4. Give me an example of a recent incident in which you took the initiative on a project.

5. Would you still take the initiative on a project if you knew you weren't going to be recognized for it?

6. Our clients frequently ask for projects to be changed midprocess. Tell me how you have dealt in the past with similar midprocess requests for project changes.

7. Describe your participation on an IT steering committee. What was the challenge? What was your role? What was the outcome?

8. With respect to your participation on an IT steering committee, what technology did you choose? Why? How did it work out?

9. Tell me about a time when you had to analyze facts quickly, define key issues, and respond immediately or develop a plan that produced good results.

Questions to Determine Fit

10. How comfortable are you with change?

11. Which computer trade journals do you find most useful? Why?

12. Have you ever made a presentation at an industry trade show or seminar?

13. Have you published anything on IT?

Core Competency Questions

14. What structured programming methodologies have you found most effective?

15. User(s) are complaining of delays when using the network. What would you do?

16. What are some of the problems associated with operating a switched LAN?

17. How do you go about monitoring and controlling the use of resources?

18. What techniques and tools can you use to ensure that a new application is as user friendly as possible?

19. What do you think is our organization's strength? Weakness?

20. How would I put my socket in nonblocking mode?

21. Tell us about a difficult or complex programming assignment you've had. What steps did you take, and how successful were you?

22. What was the most difficult programming error that you have ever encountered, and how did you solve it?

23. What actions can you take to ensure that user requirements are appropriately addressed in the implementation of a new application?

24. What is a *message queue*?

25. What is DHCP?

Ethics Questions

26. Can acting ethically increase a company's bottom line? How?

Brainteasers and Business Problems

27. How can you tell a good program from a bad one?

28. When I say the word *initiative*, what is the first thought that comes to mind?

Closing Questions

29. Do you have any questions for us?

SCRIPT 39

Sales Management

Icebreaker and Background Questions

1. Can you tell me a little about yourself?

2. What do you know about our organization?

Behavioral Questions

3. How did you go about learning a new skill that was required for your job?

4. Give an example of a situation in which you failed, and describe how you handled it.

5. What characteristics are the most important in a good manager? How have you displayed these characteristics?

6. What two or three accomplishments have given you the most satisfaction?

7. Describe a leadership role you have had, and tell me why you committed your time to it.

Questions to Determine Fit

8. What strategies have you found successful in managing unfair criticism?

9. Can you describe a time when you pushed too hard on a prospect to the detriment of a relationship?

10. If I were talking with your supervisors/subordinates/colleagues, what adjectives would they use to describe you?

Core Competency Questions

11. You'll be required to hit the ground running for this job. How will you be able to handle this?

Ethics Questions

12. What are the most common ethical problems that managers face?

Brainteasers and Business Problems

13. Do you want this job? [One hopes the answer is positive.] Then why, through our entire discussion, have you not asked for it?

14. Take as a given that you got this job and you have been doing it for three to six months, but things are just not working out. We are sitting here discussing the situation. What do you think you would say about what went wrong?

Closing Questions

15. Do you have any questions for us?

SCRIPT 40

Education, Academics, and/or Training

Icebreaker and Background Questions

1. Can you tell me a little about yourself?

2. How did you first become interested in your subject area?

Behavioral Questions

3. If I were to interview people who have been your students, how would they describe your teaching style?

4. What is your basic teaching philosophy?

5. Tell us how your research has influenced your teaching. In what ways have you been able to bring the insights of your research to your courses at the undergraduate level?

Questions to Determine Fit

6. Tell me about a time when you made a meaningful difference in the career development of a subordinate or colleague.

7. Your degree is from _____. What makes you think you would like to (or even would know how to) teach in an institution like this?

8. Why do you especially want to teach at _____? How do you see yourself contributing to our department?

Core Competency Questions

9. What do you continue to learn from teaching general survey or service courses?

10. Tell us about your research program. What are you working on currently? What do you plan to look at next?

11. You've seen our mission statement. How would you see yourself contributing to our mission and campus atmosphere?

Ethics Questions

12. Tell us about a time you handled an ethics issue. How did you resolve it?

Brainteasers and Business Problems

13. What is the cutting edge in your field, and how does your work extend it?

14. What is the broader significance of your research? How does it expand our historic understanding, literary knowledge, and/or humanistic horizons?

Closing Questions

15. Do you have any questions for us?

PART III

OTHER CRUCIAL INTERVIEW TOPICS
AND QUESTIONS

8

Acceptable and Unacceptable Personal Questions

First of all, there's no such thing as "illegal interview questions." Legislatures have not yet passed laws prohibiting some questions while permitting others. Still, while the act of asking certain types of questions is not illegal, it is often ill-advised. However, what is illegal is the act of denying employment to an individual on the basis of the answers that certain questions elicit. There are many laws, both federal and state, that make discrimination on the basis of race, gender, age, religion, sexual orientation, national heritage, and creed actionable on a number of levels. The act of asking such questions can be considered evidence of discrimination. An organization that permits its interviewers to ask discriminatory questions exposes itself to costly legal liability. Furthermore, asking discriminatory questions is just bad business practice.

Two critical lessons can be taken from this reality:

➤ First, all interview questions should be job related, and questions that are not should not be asked. If you're not sure about a question, apply this test: Does the question go to business necessity? Does the question relate to this individual candidate's ability to perform the tasks for which he or she is being considered?

➤ Second, if the answers to the questions can't be legally used, avoid the questions completely.

In the United States, the Equal Employment Opportunity Commission (EEOC) enforces laws against job discrimination, including Title VII of the Civil Rights Act of 1964, the Pregnancy Discrimination Act, the Age Discrimination in Employment Act, the Equal Pay Act, and the Americans with Disabilities Act. The EEOC publishes the *Uniform Guidelines for Employee Selection Procedures*. Over 30 states also have nondiscrimination laws. The laws governing the hiring process are complex and outside the purview of this book. The general observations offered here refer to U.S. law. Many other countries have similar requirements. It is the responsibility of anyone in a hiring position to understand these laws and how they affect the company's employment procedures and practices.

The basic point is that while the EEOC and the various state agencies are not particularly interested in the questions asked by an employer, they are vitally concerned about how the employer uses the answers to the questions. Asking dubious questions leaves companies vulnerable to discrimination lawsuits. The very act of asking such questions sets up an inference that the company will use the answers discriminatorily. It is for this reason that the HR departments of many companies enforce rules against company interviewers asking certain questions.

The interview questions below are classified as either "unacceptable" or "acceptable." Unacceptable interview questions refer to those questions asked during an interview that may be perceived to have little basis other than to discriminate against an interviewee. Interviewers need to be aware of what questions are unacceptable before they begin an interview. Some acceptable questions become unacceptable based on the reason they are asked. For example, if foreign language capability is relevant to the job at hand, it is proper to ask a candidate about language capabilities. However, the same question becomes unacceptable when it is used to gain information about a person's nationality or place of birth and foreign language capability is not relevant to the job for which the candidate is applying.

QUESTIONS

GENERAL
Unacceptable

1. What is your maiden name?

2. How much do you weigh?

3. What social or political organizations do you belong to?

4. Are you living with anyone?

5. How tall are you?

6. What ties do you have to your community?

7. If the position is offered to you, is there anyone with whom you have to discuss this offer before you make a decision?

Acceptable

1. What is your name?

2. What are you currently earning?

3. Will you be making this job decision by yourself?

MARITAL STATUS
Unacceptable

1. What is your marital status?

2. What is the name of your relative/spouse/children?

3. How old are your children?

4. What does your spouse think about your career?

5. Are you married, divorced, separated, or single?

Acceptable

1. What are the names of your relatives already employed by the company or a competitor?

2. Describe the role of your family in your career.

PREGNANCY AND CHILDREN

Unacceptable

1. Are you married?

2. Are you a single parent?

3. Do you have children?

4. Do you plan on having (any/more) children?

5. What do you use for birth control?

6. What kind of child-care arrangements have you made?

7. Who will take care of your children?

8. Are you a family man (or woman)?

9. Do you intend to get married soon?

10. What are your long-range plans for family?

11. How many people live in your household?

12. Do you live by yourself?

13. Do you have someone who can take care of a sick child?

Acceptable

Do you foresee any long-term absences in the future?

Note: Inquiries relating to duration of stay on a job or anticipated absences must be made to male and female applicants alike.

RESIDENCE

Unacceptable

1. With whom do you reside?

2. Do you live with your parents?

3. Do you own your home?

4. Do you rent your home?

5. Do you live in the city or in the suburbs?

Acceptable

1. Will you have problems getting to work by 9 a.m.?

2. May we have a current mailing address?

Note: Inquiries about address should be made only to the extent needed to facilitate contacting the applicant by mail. A post office box is a valid address.

RACE

Unacceptable

Would working with people of another race be a problem?

Acceptable

None. Asking about a person's race or color is inappropriate. Exceptions hold for employment records for an equal opportunity employer and for affirmative action status, after hiring.

CITIZENSHIP

Unacceptable

1. Are you a citizen of the United States?

2. Are your parents or spouse citizens of the United States?

3. On what dates did you, your parents, or your spouse acquire U.S. citizenship?

4. Are you, your parents, or your spouse naturalized or native-born U.S. citizens?

Acceptable

1. Are you able to provide proof of employment eligibility upon hire?

2. Can you provide proof of citizenship (passport), visa, or alien registration number after hiring?

3. If you are not a U.S. citizen, do you have the legal right to remain permanently in the United States?

4. What is your visa status (if the applicant has answered no to the previous question)?

NATIONAL ORIGIN AND/OR ANCESTRY

Unacceptable

1. Where were you born?

2. In what city/country did you grow up?

3. Where are your people from?

4. How did you acquire the ability to speak, read, or write a foreign language?

5. How did you acquire familiarity with a foreign language?

6. What language is spoken in your home?

7. What is your mother tongue?

8. That's an interesting accent. What country do you come from?

9. What was your first language?

10. What languages do your parents speak?

11. Are you bilingual?

12. What's the origin of your name?

13. What language do you speak at home?

Acceptable

What languages do you speak, read, or write fluently?

Note: The preceding question is acceptable only when the inquiry is based on a job requirement.

AGE

Unacceptable

1. How old are you?

2. When were you born?

3. How many years has it been since you graduated from college?

4. When were you married?

5. How old are your children?

6. When did you graduate from high school?

7. Would you have any difficulty working for a boss who is younger than you?

Note: It's unacceptable to ask any question that has the effect of identifying a person over 40 years old.

Acceptable

1. If hired, can you furnish proof of age?

2. Are you at least 18 years of age?

DISABILITY

Unacceptable

1. What health problems do you have?

2. Do you have any disabilities?

3. Are you physically fit and strong?

4. Is your hearing good?

5. Can you read small print?

6. Do you have any back problems?

7. Have you ever been denied health insurance?

8. When were you hospitalized the last time?

9. Is any member of your family disabled?

10. Have you ever been addicted to drugs?

11. Have you ever filed for worker's compensation?

12. Do you see a physician on a regular basis?

13. When was your last medical checkup?

14. Do you have large prescription drug bills?

15. Do you have any handicaps?

16. What caused your handicap?

17. What is the prognosis of your handicap?

18. Have you ever had any serious illness?

19. Do you have any physical disabilities?

20. Have you ever received worker's compensation?

21. Do you have problems with alcohol or drugs?

22. Do you have HIV or AIDS?

Note: It's unacceptable to ask any question that would tend to divulge handicaps or health conditions that do not relate reasonably to the level and type of fitness necessary to perform the specific job in question.

Acceptable

1. Are you capable of performing the essential responsibilities of the job?

2. Do you need any special accommodations to perform the job you've applied for?

3. Can you lift 40 pounds five feet off the ground?

4. Are you capable of driving a forklift in a warehouse with standard aisles?

5. How many days did you miss from work (or school) in the past year?

Note: To be acceptable, the preceding questions have to relate to the job.

FAMILY

Unacceptable

How will your husband feel about the amount of time you will be traveling if you get this job?

Note: Questions concerning the spouse or the spouse's employment or salary, and questions about child-care arrangements or dependents in general are unacceptable.

Acceptable

1. Can you work overtime when needed?

2. Is there any reason why you can't be on the job at 7:30 a.m.?

3. Can you work weekends?

4. Can you do shift work?

Note: Whether an applicant can meet specified work schedules or has activities or commitments that may prevent him or her from meeting attendance requirements are acceptable topics for interview questions.

GENDER AND SEX
Unacceptable

1. Do you wish to be addressed as Mr., Mrs., Miss, or Ms.?

2. Are you fertile, or do you have the capacity to reproduce?

3. What are your plans about having children in the future?

4. What's your sexual orientation?

5. Are you a member of any gay or lesbian groups?

6. Are you straight?

7. Do you date members of the opposite or same sex?

Acceptable

None.

PERSONAL FINANCES
Unacceptable

1. What is your economic situation or status?

2. What kind of car do you drive?

3. Who paid for your education?

4. Do you have debts?

5. Do you own or rent your home?

6. How much insurance do you have?

7. What is your net worth?

Acceptable

Upon our job offer, can you provide a credit report?

EDUCATION

Unacceptable

1. Did you support yourself through college?

2. Did you have a college scholarship?

Note: Any question asking specifically the nationality or the racial or religious affiliation of a school is unacceptable.

Acceptable

All questions related to academic, vocational, or professional education of an applicant, including the names of the schools attended, degrees and/or diplomas received, dates of graduation, and courses of study are acceptable.

ARRESTS AND CONVICTIONS

Unacceptable

1. Have you ever been arrested?

2. Have you ever been in prison?

Acceptable

1. Have you been convicted under criminal law within the past five years (excluding minor traffic violations)?

2. Are you currently under the supervision of a state or federal criminal justice system?

Note: It is permissible to inquire about convictions for acts of dishonesty or breach of trust. These relate to fitness to perform the particular job being applied for, as stipulated by the Federal Deposit Insurance Corporation (FDIC) requirements.

RELIGION

Unacceptable

1. This is a Christian [or Jewish or Muslim, etc.] company. Do you think you would be happy working here?

2. What's your nationality?

3. Is that an Irish [or whatever] name?

4. Would working with people of another faith be a problem?

5. Where are your parents from?

6. What is your religious affiliation?

7. Do you go to a church/synagogue/mosque?

8. Do you believe in God?

9. Do you pray?

10. What religious holidays do you observe?

11. Where are your people from?

12. Where were you born?

13. Where did you grow up?

14. Does your religion prevent you from working weekends or holidays?

15. Is that a Jewish name?

16. Is there any day of the week you're not able to work?

17. What church are you a member of?

18. Do you sing in the church choir?

19. Do your children go to Sunday school?

20. What do you do on Sundays?

21. Are you active in your church?

22. Are you a member of any religious group?

23. Are you born again?

Acceptable

This job requires work on weekends. Will that be a problem for you?

Personal Questions That Are Usually Acceptable if Asked in a Nondiscriminatory Manner

1. What should we know about you?

2. Tell me about yourself.

3. What was your favorite subject in school?

4. Did you have a favorite teacher?

5. How do you get along with people?

6. What kind of person do you get along with best?

7. What magazines do you read regularly?

8. Describe your character.

9. What's the last book you read?

10. What's the last movie you saw?

11. What do you do to stay in shape?

12. Do you have any physical problems that may limit your ability to perform this job?

13. What do you like to do when you're not at work?

14. What hobbies do you have that might help you perform in this position?

15. Are you satisfied with what you have accomplished to date?

16. What makes you angry?

17. How would your coworkers describe you?

18. How do you generally handle conflict?

19. How do you behave when you're having problems with a coworker?

20. Describe your best friend and what he or she does for a living.

21. In what ways are you similar or dissimilar to your best friend?

22. Do you like to travel?

23. What are your hobbies?

24. Are you an overachiever or an underachiever? Explain.

25. Are you an introvert or an extrovert? Explain.

26. Do you set goals for yourself?

9

Money Matters

It's a paradox. The first question that virtually all employers and candidates ask themselves is "How much money will I have to pay?" or "How much money will I get?" So one would think that a job interview would attend to the money issue straight away. But because there is a great deal of pretense concerning money, no one likes to talk about it and so it is nearly always relegated to the end of the interview. This may be inefficient, but that's the way it is.

The result is that every employment guide recommends that candidates avoid discussing salary requirements before securing real interest from the employer. The universal rule that job candidates learn is that they should do two things before even talking about money. First, they should persuade the interviewer that they are the best qualified for the job. Second, job candidates must get the interviewer to tell them the salary range of the position before they reveal how much they are making or how much they expect to earn. Thus experienced job candidates will offer all kinds of diversions designed to distract interviewers from talking about their current earning situation or expectations.

At the same time, however, the interviewers are keenly interested in getting a sense of the applicants' monetary requirements. Interviewers may be within their rights to insist on direct answers to straight questions such as "What are you earning now?" or "What's the minimum salary you will accept?" but framing the questions in such a naked fashion can blow a blast of cold air on an otherwise amiable interview. The following questions offer alternatives to get to the same information. This chapter, in addition, lists some questions related to noncash compensation.

QUESTIONS

1. Can you review your salary history for me?

2. Is money important to you?

3. I understand your reluctance to commit to a salary estimate here. However, I need to know what salary you are seeking in order to know if your salary is within our range.

4. What salary, excluding benefits, are you making now?

5. What do you expect in the way of salary for this position?

6. Why aren't you earning more at your age?

7. What do you feel this position should pay?

8. Would you consider taking less pay than you made in your last job?

9. How can we best reward you?

10. What kind of salary reviews or progress would you expect in this company?

11. In your professional opinion, what is the value added, expressed in dollars, of the position for which you are applying?

12. What do you think you're worth? Why do you think you're worth that?

13. How do you think your compensation should be determined?

14. What value can you add to our organization?

15. How much money do you want to be making five years from now?

16. How much did you make on your last job?

17. What sort of salary are you looking for?

18. Would you be willing to work for less?

19. What was the last raise you got? Were you satisfied?

20. How would you justify a raise to your current supervisor?

21. The salary you're asking for is near the top of the range for this job. Why should we pay you this much?

22. Are you able to accept a job paying less than you are currently making?

23. How would you feel if a person reporting to you made more money than you?

24. Is money the most important aspect of the job for you?

25. What do you think of a process by which subordinates have a say in the compensation of their supervisor?

26. What salary do you expect to make in this position? What do you base that figure on?

27. Have you ever worked on commission? Tell me about it.

28. Why aren't you making more money at this point in your career?

29. Are you satisfied with your salary history at this point in your career?

30. How important are stock options or deferred-payment plans to you?

31. What noncash aspects of your compensation are important to you?

32. Are you able to work on commission?

33. Are you "underemployed"?

34. Are you looking for a salary advancement?

35. What is the most important part of the compensation package a job offers?

36. Do you have a minimum salary for which you will work?

37. How do you see your salary requirements changing in the near future?

38. How important is money to you?

39. How important is overtime to you?

40. How much compensation will it take to get you here?

41. How much do you expect to be making in five years?

42. How much money do you currently make?

43. How much money do you hope to earn at age 30/35/40/45/ . . . ?

44. I can imagine you must have a specific number in mind for salary in order for you to accept the position. What is it?

45. This job might entail a cut in pay. Is this acceptable to you?

46. Why are you willing to take a cut in pay?

47. What benefits are you looking for?

48. What kind of money do you need to make?

49. What kind of salary are you looking for?

50. How much money do you eventually want to make?

51. What types of benefits does your current employer offer?

52. Which is more important to you, the money or the quality of the job?

10

Exit Interview Questions

An exit interview (or exit survey) is a conversation, usually face-to-face but sometimes in writing or in electronic feedback form, between a departing employee and a representative from the employer. The employee may be leaving either voluntarily or involuntarily. The interview can follow a structured format or be conducted on an informal basis; written questionnaires can even be used in place of a face-to-face meeting. Whichever format is used, exit interviews are generally documented.

Most employers conduct exit interviews with at least some departing employees. Employees who leave voluntarily or involuntarily are sources of valuable information. The departing employee may be much more candid than any current employee. Both parties benefit from professional exit interviews. Exit interviews are a good way for the departing employee to voice complaints, offer constructive criticism, let off steam, air some gripes, or explain why he or she is heading elsewhere. But the real value of the exit interview is most clearly for the employer, who can use it as a reality check, a trend-spotter, and an informal but significant review to evaluate the company's recruitment cycle.

Before sitting down with the departing employee, the interviewer must be clear as to the company's agenda. Does the company want the departing employee to change his or her mind and remain an employee on some mutually agreeable terms? If so, then the meeting is not precisely an exit interview. More typically, the departing employee's decision to terminate employment is final, and the purpose of the interview is to elicit candid information that can be used to fine-tune the company and the recruiting process.

With face-to-face interviews, questions beginning with "what" and "how" are best for getting departing employees to convey candid information. Some of these questions are more suitable for management employees. It's always best to give departing employees at every level an opportunity to comment on issues that may not officially be in their job description. In the event "what" and "how" questions do not provide the detail the interviewer is looking for, follow-ups with "why" questions can often elicit the desired detail.

These questions are not in any hierarchical list, although some attempt has been made to organize them logically. Some questions get at the same information using different wording. There are more questions here than anyone would normally ask in a typical exit interview. Select the questions and wordings that are most relevant to the leaving circumstances, the interviewee, and your organization situation.

QUESTIONS

1. Tell me about how you've come to decide to leave.

2. What is your primary reason for leaving?

3. Are there any other reasons for your leaving?

4. Why is this decision important or significant for you?

5. Within the context of [particular reason to leave], what was it that concerned you most?

6. What could have been done early on to prevent the situation from escalating to this point?

7. How would you have preferred the situation(s) to have been handled?

8. What opportunities can you see that might have existed for the situation/problems to have been addressed satisfactorily?

9. What was most satisfying about your job?

10. What was least satisfying about your job?

11. What would you change about your job?

12. Did your job duties turn out to be as you expected?

13. Did you receive enough training to do your job effectively?

14. Did you receive adequate support to do your job?

15. Did you receive sufficient feedback about your performance between merit reviews?

16. How do you feel about the organization?

17. Did this company help you to fulfill your career goals?

18. Do you have any tips to help us find your replacement?

19. Were you satisfied with this company's merit review process?

20. What would you improve to make our workplace better?

21. Were you happy with your pay, benefits, and other incentives?

22. What was the quality of the supervision you received?

23. What could your immediate supervisor do to improve his or her management style?

24. Based on your experience with us, what do you think it takes to succeed at this company?

25. Did any company policies or procedures (or any other obstacles) make your job more difficult?

26. What can you say about the processes and procedures or systems that have contributed to the problem(s)/your decision to leave?

27. What specific suggestions would you have for how the organization could manage this situation/these issues better in the future?

28. What has been good/enjoyable/satisfying for you in your time with us?

29. What has been frustrating/difficult/upsetting to you in your time with us?

30. What could you have done better or more for us had we given you the opportunity?

31. What extra responsibility would you have welcomed that you were not given?

32. How could the organization have enabled you to make fuller use of your capabilities and potential?

33. Would you consider working again for this company in the future?

34. Would you recommend working for this company to your family and friends?

35. How do you generally feel about this company?

36. What did you like most about this company?

37. What did you like least about this company?

38. What does your new company offer that this company doesn't?

39. Can this company do anything to encourage you to stay?

40. Before deciding to leave, did you investigate a transfer within the company?

41. Did anyone in this company discriminate against you, harass you, or cause hostile working conditions for you? Any other comments?

42. What could you say about communications and relations between departments, and how could these be improved?

43. What training would you have liked or needed that you did not get, and what effect would this have had?

44. How well do you think your training and development needs were assessed and met?

45. What training and development did you find most helpful and enjoyable?

46. Can you tell me about a situation with a customer you dealt with that didn't go too well, and what you would now do differently?

47. What improvements do you think can be made to customer service and relations?

48. How would you describe the culture of the organization?

49. Were you oriented adequately for your role(s)?

50. What improvement could be made to the way that you were inducted/prepared for your role(s)?

51. What can you say about the way your performance was measured and the feedback you received on your performance results?

52. What suggestion would you make to improve working conditions, hours, shifts, amenities, and so on?

53. How well do you think the appraisal system worked for you?

54. What would you say about how you were motivated, and how that could have been improved?

55. What can you say about the way you were managed? On a day-to-day basis? And on a month-to-month basis?

56. How would you have changed the expectations/objectives/aims (or absence of) that were placed on you? Why?

57. What, if any, examples of ridiculous policies, rules, and/or instructions can you highlight?

58. What examples of ridiculous waste (material or effort), pointless reports, meetings, bureaucracy, and so on, could you point to?

59. How could the organization reduce stress levels among employees where stress is an issue?

60. How could the organization have enabled you to have made better use of your time?

61. What things did the organization or management do to make your job more difficult/frustrating/nonproductive?

62. Aside from the reason(s) you are leaving, how strongly were you attracted to committing to a long and developing career with us?

63. What can the organization do to retain its best people (and not lose any more like you)?

64. Have you anything to say about your treatment from a discrimination or harassment perspective?

65. Would you consider working again for us if the situation were right?

Exit Interview Questions for Recent Recruits Who Have Stayed in the Position for a Year or Less

66. How could you have been helped to better know/understand/work with other departments necessary for the organization to perform more effectively?

67. How could we have improved your own recruitment?

68. How could your induction training have been improved?

69. How did the reality alter from your expectations when you first joined us?

11

Questions Interviewers Should Expect to Be Asked

I f a candidate has not conducted a due diligence on the firm and its key staff, then you know that either the candidate does not know the information exists or he or she has not had the interest or commitment to look for it, or both. In either case, it's indicative of a mindset that might drop the candidate significantly in your estimation. On the other hand, more and more candidates do ask questions, sometimes very challenging questions. Be prepared to respond to questions such as the following.

QUESTIONS

About the Position

1. Why is the position open?

2. Is this a newly created position? How long has the position been open?

3. What happened to the person who previously held this position?

4. How many employees have held this position in the last three years?

5. How long has this position existed in the organization? Has its scope changed recently?

6. What's your "call to action" for employees?

7. What's your ideal employee like?

8. Imagine that I excel in this position. Where would I go from here?

9. Can you give me an idea of the typical day on the job and its workload and special demands?

10. How does an employee succeed on your team?

11. What will be my first assignment?

12. What tasks will fill a majority of my time?

13. What challenges do you think I will face in this position?

14. Could you show me a formal job description?

15. What can I bring Company XYZ to round out the team?

16. By what criteria will you select the person for this job?

17. Where does this position fit into the organization?

18. What kind of person are you looking for?

19. When was the last person promoted?

20. What is the ideal experience and skill set for this position?

21. What problems might I expect to encounter on this job?

22. What is the normal salary range for this job?

23. Tell me about promotions and advancement in this company.

24. What are your expectations of the person hired for this job?

25. What are the three most significant things that need to be accomplished by the person in this position in the first year, and what major hurdles will that person encounter?

26. Can you tell me more about what my day-to-day responsibilities would be?

27. Who has the final say in this hiring decision?

28. How much freedom would I have to determine my work objectives and deadlines?

29. What kind of support does this position receive in terms of people and resources?

30. How would my performance be measured, and how is successful performance usually rewarded?

31. Can you give me a formal, written description of the position? I'm interested in reviewing in detail the major activities involved and what results are expected.

32. Can you please tell me a little bit about the people with whom I'll be working most closely?

33. If I were a spectacular success in this position after six months, what would I have accomplished?

34. Do you foresee significant amounts of overtime or work on weekends involved with this job?

35. If you hired me, what would be my first assignment?

36. What goals or objectives need to be achieved in the next six months?

37. How do you see this position impacting on the achievement of those goals?

38. What is the first assignment you intend to give me? Where does that assignment rank on the departmental priorities? What makes this assignment a great opportunity?

About the Management

39. How does this company go about solving problems?

40. To whom would I report? What should I know about him or her?

41. How much supervision will I get as a new employee?

42. Can you briefly tell me about the managers who will supervise me?

43. How many people will I supervise? What are their backgrounds?

44. What are the most critical factors for success in your segment of the business?

45. Are my tasks limited to my job description, or will I be performing duties outside the described job scope?

46. How much scope will I have in pursuing opportunities and initiatives beyond the job description that I believe will advance the mission of the team?

About the Company

47. What are the organization's most important goals?

48. What are your plans for company expansion?

49. What are the company's growth plans for the next five years?

50. Describe the performance evaluation procedures you use.

51. Is there anything else I should know about this company?

52. Can you describe the work environment here?

53. How do you describe the philosophy of the company or organization?

54. What do you consider to be the organization's strengths and weaknesses?

55. Assuming I was hired and performed well for a period of time, what additional opportunities might this job lead to?

56. Do the most successful people in the company tend to come from one area of the company, such as sales or engineering, or do they rise from a cross section of functional areas?

57. What's the makeup of the team as far as experience? Am I going to be a mentor, or will I be mentored?

58. What does this company value the most, and how do you think my work for you will further these values?

59. What kinds of processes are in place to help me work collaboratively?

60. Does this company typically promote from within?

61. Why are you not filling this position from within?

62. How does this position and/or department fit into the organizational structure?

63. You said I could expect to make more money down the road. When will I get a review, and what exactly will I need to do to be successful?

64. When can I expect to hear from you about the next stage in the interviewing process?

65. What major problems are we facing right now in this department or position?

66. How does upper management perceive this division or part of the organization?

67. Could you explain the company's organizational structure?

68. What is the organization's plan for the next five years, and how does this department or division fit in?

69. Will we be expanding or bringing on new products or new services that I should be aware of?

70. What are some of the skills and abilities you see as necessary for someone to succeed in this job?

71. What challenges might I encounter if I take on this position?

72. What are your major concerns that need to be immediately addressed in this job?

73. What are the department's goals, and how do they align with the company's mission?

74. What are the company's strengths and weaknesses compared with the competition [naming one or two companies]?

75. How does the reporting structure work here? What are the preferred means of communication?

76. What's the gross profit margin of the division I will be working in? What percentage of the total profit from the company does it generate? Is it increasing or decreasing?

77. What's your company's "killer application"? What percentage of the market share does it have? Will I be working on it?

78. How will my performance be evaluated? What are the top criteria you use?

79. What percentage of my compensation is based on my performance?

80. Is there a process whereby the employees get to evaluate their supervisor?

81. Is the company's training strategy linked to the company's core business objectives?

82. Are there formal metrics in place for measuring and rewarding performance over time?

83. How effectively has the company communicated its top three business goals?

About the Culture

84. How would you describe the corporate culture at this location?

85. What management style is most prevalent here?

86. How would you describe the ethical foundation for the company?

87. How are executives normally addressed by their subordinates?

88. What can you tell me about the prevailing management style?

89. Does the company have a mission statement? May I see it?

90. How does the firm handle recognition for a job well done?

91. When was the last time you rewarded a subordinate for his or her efforts? What token of appreciation did you offer?

92. What are the greatest challenges I will face in this position in furthering the values of the organization?

93. How does the firm recognize and learn from a brave attempt that didn't turn out quite as expected?

94. Does this company typically have a reactive or proactive strategy to dealing with problems?

95. I am a hard worker. I expect to be around other hard-working people. Am I going to be comfortable with the level of effort I find here?

96. Work-life balance is an issue of retention as well as productivity. Can you talk about your own view of how to navigate the tensions between getting the work done and encouraging healthy lives outside the office?

97. How does the company support and promote personal and professional growth?

98. Can you give me some examples of the best and worst aspects of the company's culture?

99. What makes this company a great place to work? What outside evidence (rankings or awards) do you have to prove this is a great place to work? What is the company going to do in the next year to make it better?

100. Your competitors all have great products and people programs. What is the deciding factor that makes this opportunity superior? Are you willing to make me some specific "promises" on what you will do to make this a great experience if I accept the position?

101. Can you show me that the company has a diverse workforce and that it is tolerant of individual differences? Does it have affinity groups or similar programs that I might find beneficial? Is there a dress code?

102. Can you give me an example of any "outrageous conduct" this firm tolerates that the competitors would not?

103. Does the company have a program to significantly reward individuals who develop patents and/or great products? Is there a program to help individuals "start" their own firms or subsidiary? Will I be required to fill out noncompete agreements?

104. How many approvals would it take (and how long) to get a new $110,000 project idea of mine approved? What percentage of employee-initiated projects in this job was approved last year?

About the Interviewer

105. What have you liked most about working for this company?

106. How did you get into your profession?

107. What are some of the problems that keep you up at night?

108. What do you see as the most important opportunities for improvement in the area I hope to join?

109. What attracted you to work for this organization?

110. What attracted you to this company, and what do you think are its strengths and weaknesses?

111. What have you liked most about working here? Least?

112. In what ways has the experience surprised or disappointed you?

113. What is the best or toughest question I could ask you in order to find out about the most troubling aspects of this job? How would you answer it?

114. If you were my best friend, what would you tell me about this job that we haven't already discussed?

115. Are there any aspects of my background or skills that you would like to hear more about?

116. What specific skills from the person you hire would make your life easier?

117. What would be a surprising but positive thing the new person could do in the first 90 days?

About the Hiring Process

118. How long will it take for you (and the company) to make a hiring decision for this position?

119. If I do a great/bad job in the first 90 days, specifically how will you let me know? What steps would you take to help me improve? How do you discipline team members?

120. Can we schedule a performance review in three months?

12

20 Very Tough Questions

When you want to salt your upcoming interview with one or two truly challenging questions, select from among these zingers.

QUESTIONS

1. Tell me about yourself using words of only one syllable.

2. Have you done the best work you are capable of?

3. What was the most useful criticism you ever received?

4. Describe the best person you have ever worked for or who has worked for you.

5. If your last boss were able to wave a magic wand over your head, what aspect of your performance would he or she fine-tune?

6. If you had the opportunity to do the last 10 years of your career over again, what would you do differently?

7. Describe the most difficult decision you have ever had to make. Reflecting back, was your decision the best possible choice you could have made? Why or why not?

8. If I were to speak with your current supervisor, what would he or she say are your current strengths and weaknesses?

9. Take as a given that you got this job, and you have been doing it for three to six months but things are just not working out. We are sitting here discussing the situation. What do you think you would say about what went wrong?

10. When you've had a really good day at work and you go home and kick back and you feel satisfied, what was it about that day that made you feel really good? When you have had a really bad day at work and you go home and feel upset, what was it about that day that made you feel really upset?

11. What cherished management belief have you had to give up in order to get where you are?

12. What's more important to you, truth or comfort?

13. Have you learned more from your mistakes or from your successes?

14. Is honesty always the best policy?

15. How has your tolerance for accepting mistakes from your subordinates changed over the years?

16. Where do you think the power comes from in your organization? Why?

17. On what occasions are you tempted to lie?

18. Is the customer always right?

19. If you could organize the world in one of three ways—no scarcity, no problems, or no rules—how would you do it?

20. Should all business relationships have fixed terms—that is, expiration dates?

13

Questions to Help Identify Applicants Who May Be Disgruntled or Prone to Violence

Workplaces throughout the nation have become battlegrounds for physical violence. An average of 1.9 million people were victims of violent crime while on duty in the United States, according to a report published by the Bureau of Justice Statistics. In 2003, there were 1,071 Americans murdered at work and 160,000 physically assaulted, according to a study by the National Institute for Occupational Safety and Health (NIOSH). The average cost to employers of a single episode of workplace violence can exceed $250,000 in lost work and legal expenses, according to the National Safe Workplace Institute.

Research on workplace violence suggests that there is a personality profile into which most candidates prone to violence fit. This profile usually includes these traits: a lack of self-esteem, poor impulse control, and a sense of victimization. This chapter lists a number of questions that, when combined with a scrupulous preemployment screening process, may be helpful in identifying candidates with these attitudes. Of course, not all candidates who have some or even all of these traits act out violently. There is no formula. It's the job of a trained interviewer to make an assessment based on the candidate's total presentation.

Most of the questions in this chapter focus on the candidate's identification with the victim role. The common thread among many incidents of workplace violence is a perpetrator's feelings of victimization. These candidates harbor perceptions that they were treated unjustly or disrespect-fully by their coworkers or supervisors or both. What's more, if you ask the questions in a relaxed, interested manner, without a hint of judgment, many applicants will offer their stories. That's because most troubled appli-cants feel that if they just tell the interviewer the facts as they perceive them, the interviewer will accept that the applicants were, indeed, the vic-tims of injustice. The interviewer has to assess such responses on a case-by-case basis.

Prescreening, combined with reference checks and personality tests, is a company's best strategy for minimizing workplace violence. An expe-rienced interviewer can use the interview process to identify temperamental candidates: those who exhibit evidence of short fuses or thin skins. There are no guarantees in the hiring process. If there were, there would be no need for this book or, in fact, 90 percent of the human resources profes-sion. The details—legal and otherwise—of screening candidates for a safe workplace are beyond the scope of this book. Nevertheless, as part of a well-considered screening program, the following interview questions can help interviewers identify candidates who may be inclined to violence.

QUESTIONS

1. Tell me about a time when your employer was not happy with your job performance.

2. Have you ever had to work with a manager who was unfair to you or who was just plain hard to work with?

3. How would you define a *difficult* manager?

4. Have you ever been in a dispute with a supervisor? What was it about, and how was it resolved?

5. How would you finish this sentence: Most people are basically . . . ?

6. Can we check your references?

7. What kind of references do you think your previous employer will give you? Why?

8. How do you deal with coworkers or supervisors who do not show you proper respect?

9. What causes you to lose your temper?

10. Describe a situation in which your work was criticized.

11. Describe how you have responded when your work has been criticized.

12. How would your subordinates describe you?

13. Tell us about the last time you lost your temper.

14. What situations make you lose your temper?

15. Tell us about the worst supervisor you've worked under.

16. Tell us about the best supervisor you've worked under.

17. Tell us about a confrontation that you've had with a coworker.

18. How do you maintain an effective working relationship with your coworkers?

19. How would your best friend describe you?

20. How would your worst enemy describe you?

21. How do you handle rejection?

22. What are some of your pet peeves?

23. Which of your skills can stand improvement at this time?

24. What problems do you have getting along with others?

25. What are some of the things your supervisor did that you disliked?

26. Were you ever dismissed from a job for a reason that seemed unjustified?

27. What kinds of things do you worry about?

28. What are some of the things that bother you?

29. If I were to call your supervisor today, how would he or she describe you?

30. Can you identify some weaknesses for which you need to compensate?

31. What do you do when your boss loads you down with a great deal of work and not enough time to do it in?

32. What do you do when there is a decision to be made and no procedure exists?

33. Are you generally lucky or unlucky?

34. We all know that family members tend to be critical of each other. Do your family members criticize you?

35. If you were going to be fired, how would you like your supervisor to handle it?